The Panic Attack, Anxiety & Phobia Solutions Handbook

by

Muriel K. MacFarlane, RN, MA

United Research Publishers

Published by United Research Publishers
Copyright ©1997 by United Research Publishers
ISBN 1-887053-00-X
Library of Congress Catalog Card Number 95-60774
Printed and bound in the United States of America

The information in this book is not intended to replace the advice of your physician. You should consult your doctor concerning any medical condition which concerns you. The material presented in this book is intended to inform and educate the reader with a view to making some intelligent choices in pursuing the goal of living your life in a healthy, vigorous manner. Neither the author nor the publisher assumes any responsibility or liability for the judgements or decisions any reader might make as a result of reading this publication.

Book design by The Final Draft, Encinitas, CA

Cover design by The Art Department, Encinitas, CA

Order additional copies from:

United Research Publishers
P.O. Box 232344
Encinitas, CA 92023-2344

Full 30-day money back guarantee if not satisfied.

CONTENTS

Introduction

FEAR. . .HEART PALPITATIONS. . .TERROR, a sense of impending doom. . .dizziness. . .fear of fear. These are the words most often used to describe panic disorder and they are very frightening. It is estimated that four to ten million individuals in the United States suffer from debilitating panic attacks. Women in their child-bearing years are the most frequent victims of this intense anxiety.

But there is great hope: VIRTUALLY EVERYONE WHO HAS THIS CONDITION CAN CONTROL AND END IT!

The encouraging progress in the understanding of panic disorder reflects recent, rapid advances in scientific understanding of the brain and body chemistry.

The President and the U.S. Congress, recognizing many of the problems of modern day citizens, have declared the 1990s the Decade of the Brain. The National Institute of Mental Health (NIMH), the Federal agency responsible for conducting and supporting research related to mental health and the brain, is conducting a nationwide education program on panic disorder during this decade. The program's purpose is to educate the public and health care professionals about the disorder, and encourage people with it to obtain help. One of the effects of such an undertaking is that the physician in general practice and the doctor in the emergency room, two of the people who often see panic attack sufferers when they have their first panic attack, will become better informed, will have more knowledge and information and thus, will consider the possibility of a panic disorder when they see someone with those frightening and bewildering symptoms.

In the United States, 1.6 percent of the adult population, or more than 3 million people, will have panic disorder at some time in their lives. The disorder typically begins in young adulthood, but older people and children can be affected. Women are affected twice as frequently as men. While people of all races and social classes can have panic disorder, there appear to be cultural differences in how individual symptoms are expressed.

Although panic disorder manifests itself with some of the most frightening and bewildering symptoms a person can experience, it is ONE OF THE MOST TREATABLE CONDITIONS. It is also one of the most common. Several studies suggest that as many as eight percent of patients seeing non-psychiatric physicians for mental consultation have panic disorder.

Panic disorder is not a new phenomenon: it has been known through history as "housewife's disease" and "soldier's heart."

Hippocrates (460-377 B.C.) described a man who had a phobia about heights and who could not cross over bridges or even stand beside a shallow ditch. In *Anatomy of Melancholy* (1621) Robert Burton described phobias:

> "There was a patient who would not walk alone for fear he would die. A second man fears that every man he meets will rob him, quarrel with him, or kill him. A third dares not venture out alone for fear he would be sick. . .another dares not go over a bridge, near a pool, brook, lie in a chamber with cross-beams, for fear he will be tempted to hang himself. If he be at a sermon, he is afraid he will speak aloud something unfit to be said. If he is locked in a closed room, he is afraid he will suffocate."

Burton also identified phobic figures from history such as Augustus Caesar, who was afraid of the dark and Demosthenes and Tully, who were afraid of public speaking. Such descriptions in history are commonplace. A contemporary of James I of England said that his fear of swords was so great that Elizabeth was King, James I was Queen.

In 1721, a physician described individuals with phobias of syphilis:

> "So strongly are they possessed with this notion that an honest practitioner generally finds it more difficult to cure the imaginary evil than the real one."

Sigmund Freud had many anxiety symptoms, including his well documented fear of travel.

The author Edgar Allan Poe was very famous for his claustrophobia and turned his real-life fear into his classic tales of terror. He used these feelings of extreme fear to write several well-known stories such as "The Premature Burial," dwelling on a common fear and putting it into words so that all could experience the terror of being buried alive he probably felt himself.

We can see that this has been a common human condition, affecting not only the ordinary person but the famous and the rich, who, despite their fame and their wealth, probably got little help to end their suffering.

That was then--this is now.

What is new is our understanding of panic disorder and what to do about it.

By reading this book you will gain a clear and simple understanding of just how panic disorder begins, how it develops, and most importantly what you can do to help yourself and cure it. By following the advice in this book you can help yourself to live a full and satisfying life, no longer crippled by this debilitating illness.

TO THINK IS TO PRACTICE BODY CHEMISTRY.

THERE IS A MOLECULAR RESPONSE WITHIN YOUR BODY TO EVERY THOUGHT

and once you understand just how this works and the effect it has on your life, you can begin to change for the better.

YOU CANNOT CHANGE THE PAST--YOU WILL LIVE THE REST OF YOUR LIFE IN THE FUTURE.

But, you can change how you let the past affect you and you can make changes for the future that will make anxiety, phobias and panic attacks just part of your past.

Read on. . .for RELIEF FROM PANIC ATTACKS!

PART I

What is Wrong with Me?

Chapter I
Overcome by Fear

Terror on the Train

Sandra was only 22 when she had her first full-blown panic attack on her way home from work. It was a cool autumn evening, and just like millions of other young women who work daily in the downtown area of her city, she was dressed for the office, wearing a silk blouse and a single strand of beads around her neck. She had swung easily onto the train for the ride home, found a seat and opened her paperback book as she settled into her seat. She had done this hundreds of times before and nothing on this day seemed any different than any other work day.

"Suddenly, I felt just as if I was going to pass out. I couldn't breathe, my heart was racing. I could feel the sweat running down the inside of my sleeves. In a matter of minutes my blouse was soaked through and sticking to my skin. I thought I was choking or having a heart attack. I clawed at my neck, breaking my necklace and scattering the beads everywhere. I just knew I was going to die. I began to look around wildly. I don't know what the other passengers thought but I could see they were moving away from me, startled looks on their faces. I could hear someone screaming--'Get an ambulance!'--and I realized it was me.

"We weren't anywhere near my station but I gathered some strength from somewhere and bolted off the train when the doors opened. It was a relief to get out in the cool air even if it was an unfamiliar depot. I began to feel better as soon as I was off the train and I sat down to collect myself. I sat there for a long time. 'Was it just too hot on the train? Were there too many people crowding close to me, invading my space? It is like that every day, so what's the difference?'"

When the next train came, Sandra got on and headed home. "By the time I got home it was just like a bad dream. I was so embarrassed by the whole thing I just didn't tell anyone, I would have felt too foolish."

But Sandra's evening of terror was just the beginning. Her life was turning into a living nightmare.

"Doctor, am I having a heart attack?"

Panic disorder is a debilitating condition that may afflict as many as 3 million people in the course of a lifetime. This disorder is characterized by panic attacks, which are sudden bursts of terror which seem to come out of nowhere.

According to the National Institute of Mental Health, approximately 10 percent of all people will have a panic attack at some time in their lives. But victims of full-blown panic disorder can experience four or more panic attacks every month.

People suffering from a panic attack often think they are having a heart attack or that they are going insane.

After four or five visits to the local emergency room and several visits to doctors and specialists where they are given a battery of tests, including blood work, a twenty-four hour heart monitoring test, a brain scan and numerous x-rays, panic disorder sufferers are often told there is absolutely nothing wrong with them. Instead of feeling a sense of relief on hearing such a diagnosis, the patient goes away KNOWING that something is very wrong but not what. It is terrible to know something is very wrong and still feel that the doctor thinks you are nothing but a "head case."

The next time the panic strikes, most people are reluctant to seek any medical help for fear of getting the same diagnosis and the same treatment.

According to Francis J. Kane, Jr., a professor of psychiatry at Baylor College of Medicine and a physician at Houston's Methodist Hospital, hundreds of people suffer from severe chest pain that is caused by anxiety or panic disorder rather than heart disease. These people often receive inadequate or inappropriate medical care once doctors determine that their hearts are healthy, and they sometimes become crippled by the belief that they have heart disease, in spite of their physician's reassurances.

Studies have shown that primary care physicians seldom diagnose panic disorders and even heart specialists seldom diagnose panic disorder when examining patients with chest pain.

500,000 individuals undergo diagnostic cardiac catheterization each year, and about one third of them have normal coronary arteries. Another one half or more of these people continue to believe they have heart disease. They experience chest pain, continue to use heart medications, and have a lowered capacity to carry out daily activities. It is suggested that almost half of patients with normal coronary arteries may be suffering panic disorder. Over a three to four year period, follow-up found these patients still had chest pain, poor health, less exercise capacity, more symptoms of anxiety and psychological distress.

A study conducted at Harvard's Massachusetts General Hospital found that 70 percent of panic attack patients had been to more than ten physicians each before they were diagnosed correctly! Usually these poor individuals were labeled neurotics who were suffering from a variety of ailments including hysteria, hypochondria or cardiac neurosis, or other conditions that reflected the specialty or the particular bias of the physician conducting the examination.

"Doctor, I think I'm losing my mind."

The statistics indicate that among women, anxiety ranks as the number one psychiatric disorder in all age groups, and mental health experts agree. It is not that men don't ever suffer from anxiety, it is just that they are less likely than women to seek professional help. Instead, men tend to ignore the problem, or turn to alcohol to control their panic. Studies at the National Institute of Mental Health show that alcohol abuse is twice as common among men as women, and that as many as one-third to one-half of all alcoholics suffer from undiagnosed and untreated phobias or panic disorders.

What is Anxiety?

Anxiety is nothing more than a feeling of apprehension and uncertainty. We have all felt that--when we take a test, no matter how well prepared we might be; when we go for a job interview, no matter how right we think we might be for the position; when we find ourselves driving on an unfamiliar road in a rainstorm, no matter how good a driver we might think we are. This is a very normal reaction to something that is unfamiliar and which might have an outcome that we don't expect or won't like. This kind of uncertainty is helpful: it puts us on the alert. It tunes up our muscles and our brains to be prepared to handle the unexpected.

This kind of anxiety is not helpful if it makes us so anxious that we are unable to take the test or remember the answers; if we can't talk at the interview and so present ourselves in a bad light; if we lose control of the car we are driving because we tighten up and oversteer.

But to live without anxiety is impossible. It can be an exhausting stress or a stimulating tonic. It has many degrees of intensity. The professional public speaker sees it as giving him an "edge" so that he entertains and holds his audience. Many of the rest of us see speaking in public as so terrifying that we avoid it at all costs.

Anxiety and fear are often used interchangeably without really expressing the difference between them.

A phobia is a kind of anxiety yet it is defined as "a persistent or irrational fear." One may complain of being anxious in anticipation of a specific event such as public speaking but will say one is "terrified of public speaking." Others question that, since they say "What could happen that could be so frightening?"

Anxiety seems to be caused by concerns which are external to the individual, while phobia can be viewed as an extreme response to a less obvious, ill-defined, distant, or unrecognized source of danger. Anxiety describes an unpleasant state of mental tension often accompanied by physical or psychological symptoms, in which the sufferer feels both physically and mentally helpless, exhausted by always being on guard against the anticipated danger.

An anxious person is apprehensive and continually feels worried, ruminates and anticipates that something unpleasant will happen. The individual feels "on edge," impatient or irritable. This sounds familiar because it is a human condition to be anxious some of the time but the question is: Where does "normal" anxiety end and "abnormal" anxiety begin? Where does mere concern change and become marked discomfort or extremely intense panic?

The answer to that question is complex. Some of the answer lies in an understanding of how our nervous system works, how our personalities are formed, and how we view the world around us. And what we do to respond to our nervous system's signals.

The Way the Nervous System Works

The nervous system has two main divisions, the voluntary and the involuntary. It isn't absolutely necessary to understand the working of the nervous system, but you might want to read for a better understanding of the WHY of the symptoms of panic disorders.

The Voluntary System

The voluntary nervous system is relatively simple to understand. The brain and the spinal cord make up this system, with a number of paired nerves arising from the spine and ending in a muscle. When we think a thought to direct our limbs, head and body, we control the movement of these body parts voluntarily. If we think to hold our hand still, for instance, then our hand will lie motionless in our lap.

The Involuntary System

The involuntary system controls the operation of our heart, lungs, intestines and various other internal systems. We don't have to think about it for our heart to continue beating and even if we try, we cannot stop it from beating--it is under the control of our involuntary nerves which send out messages controlled by our endocrine glands. These glands respond to things we think are happening in our environment.

For example, if you are in a group of people who are relatively unfamiliar to you and someone tells a crude joke which makes you uncomfortable, you might find yourself blushing. If someone in the group says, "Oh, look, she's blushing!" you might find you are blushing even more, much as you would prefer not to. You also might look around and find that everyone else is laughing at the joke--you are the only one embarrassed by it.

Your glands have sent a chemical message to your involuntary nervous system based on how YOU perceived the situation. The involuntary system has two parts, the sympathetic and the parasympathetic.

Parasympathetic

The parasympathetic division is concerned with activities that restore and conserve bodily energy. For instance, under normal conditions, parasympathetic impulses to the digestive glands (which control the smooth muscles of the digestive system) dominate over sympathetic impulses. This allows energy-supplying foods to be digested and absorbed by the body.

Sympathetic

The sympathetic division, by contrast, is concerned with processes involving the expenditure of energy. When everything is normal, the main function of the sympathetic division is to counteract the parasympathetic effects just enough to carry out normal processes that require energy.

However, during a time of stress, the sympathetic dominates the parasympathetic. For example, when confronted with a dangerous situation, a person becomes very alert because fear stimulates the sympathetic division. This causes the pupils of the eyes to dilate, the heart rate to increase, the blood vessels of the skin and the intestines to constrict, and the remainder of the blood vessels to dilate. This, in turn, causes a rise in blood pressure and a faster flow of blood into the dilated vessels of the skeletal muscles, cardiac muscle, the lungs, and the brain--organs that are involved in fighting off danger.

Rapid breathing occurs as the bronchioles dilate to allow movement of air in and out of the lungs at a faster rate. Blood sugar levels rise as the liver converts glycogen to glucose to supply the additional energy needed. The adrenals produce epinephrine, a hormone that intensifies and prolongs these effects.

During this period of stress, the sympathetic effects inhibit other processes that are not essential for meeting the situation. For example, muscular movements of the gastrointestinal tract and digestive secretions are slowed down or even stopped.

The nervous system reacts to stimuli quickly and produces responses by almost instantaneous electrical conduction over its pathways. The parasympathetic system reacts more slowly and produces changes by releasing chemicals (hormones) into the bloodstream.

The parasympathetic system is governed by the endocrine glands, which produce hormones. These glands are the pituitary, thyroid, parathyroids, adrenals, pancreas, ovaries, testes, pineal and the thymus.

The Pattern of Response

Because our bodies are very complex chemical factories, producing hundreds of chemicals which control a great variety of bodily functions, it would not be improbable to find that some of these chemicals are slightly out of balance in many of us.

Some people are tall, some are short, some produce more of one hormone, others less. There is nothing wrong about any of these things; it is a matter of genetics just how our bodies are constructed and how they function.

When a couple produces a child, their genetics come together to produce a new combination. In this new human being's combination there can be a minute, almost imperceptible imbalance.

A variety of researchers believe that people who get panic attacks tend to have minor abnormalities in the brain's limbic system, one of its emotional centers. Other researchers believe that the brain's chemistry, especially the portion that regulates alertness, may be out of kilter since many panic patients are hypervigilant about their bodily functions and have a general sense of helplessness--patterns that feed the disorder.

Says Dr. James Ballanger, chairman of the psychiatry department at the Medical University of South Carolina and a board member of the Anxiety Disorders Association of America: "Everybody has an alarm reaction in their brain--we'd all panic if we were drowning. But for the panic disorder sufferers, that alarm rheostat is set too tight."

When looking at the genetic predisposition, Robert Moreines, M.D., associate director of New Jersey's Princeton Psychiatric Center, says, "We have been looking at young children of mothers with panic disorders, and these kids are shy and clinging and have difficulty separating. There seems to be an innate vulnerability, a certain temperament that they are born with."

Other experts suggest that anxiety disorders originate in conflicts or distress dating back to child-hood. "Every single person I've seen with an anxiety disorder has been traumatized in childhood," says New York City psychotherapist Janet Damon, "It hasn't been necessarily gross abuse, but some sort of dys-function in the family."

If we look at and join those two suppositions:

(1) a biochemical imbalance,

AND

(2) an anxiety personality;

then we have gone a long way to understanding just why so many people suffer from anxiety related dif-ficulties, and more importantly, how to go about re-solving them.

If anxiety, and the disorders that eventually re-sult from anxiety, can be brought about by very small biochemical abnormalities in the brain's chemistry in an individual whose personality then is impacted by this biochemistry--then it is a very real physical condition for which there are very real and appropri-ate responses. In other words--anxiety, panic attacks and phobias ARE TREATABLE. THERE IS A SOLU-TION.

The Adrenaline Response

The sympathetic nervous system produces hormones, and one of those is adrenaline.

The "alarm" reaction or "fight-or-flight" response is the initial reaction of the body to any stress. It is actually a complex of reactions initiated by the stimulation of the sympathetic nervous system. It suspends all non-essential activity in the body and increases activity in any system that would be used to either fight or flee.

The responses are immediate and are designed to counteract a danger by mobilizing the body's resources for immediate physical activity. The alarm reaction brings tremendous amounts of glucose and oxygen to the organs that are most active in warding off danger. These are the brain, which must become highly alert; the skeletal muscles, which may have to fight off a strong attacker; and the heart, which must work furiously to pump enough blood and oxygen to the brain and the muscles.

In addition, it constricts the peripheral blood vessels near the surface of the body, raising the blood pressure and makes the skin appear pale; suspends digestive activity (including the flow of saliva) and in stopping this activity rechannels the blood used in this process to provide additional blood for the motor muscles; triggers the emptying of the bladder and bowels to free the body for strenuous activity.

This fight-or-flight response triggers the release of increased amounts of adrenaline (epinephrine) and related chemicals into the bloodstream. They provide additional strength, stamina, and the ability to respond rapidly. These chemicals aid soldiers to survive in battle, athletes to perform better, and all individuals to respond more effectively when faced with dangerous situations.

Our ancestors roamed the earth searching for food. Danger could lurk anywhere and these hunters and gatherers were alert for any predator coming toward them through the brush. The "fight-or-flight" response helped these early humans stay alive. If they came face to face with a hungry bear they became immediately prepared--either to do battle or to escape.

After the cave man did one or the other and managed to still be alive, he went back to hunting and gathering, his primary need--food--to be met in order to continue to stay alive. Sometimes he would find a small animal such as a rabbit or a bird. He would become the predator and the small animal the prey. That small animal would also have this "fight-or-flight" response to the arrival of the human. This "fight-or-flight" alarm response is a primary warning instinct which we share with other animals. It is a very basic survival technique and a valuable one.

Today we don't have to worry about hungry bears but we still have a lot to worry about. And worry we do. We face stress and sometimes fear from thieves, muggers, jobs, traffic, relationships and money--just to name a few. However, in our modern technological world we face very few physical dangers that require strenuous action.

Most of the threats we face today are psychological threats such as the loss of love, status, prestige and/or a sense of belonging and significance. Usually these losses do not require an immediate physical response.

And--we can't fight or run most of the time. We certainly can't run away from our jobs and expect them to be there the next day, and we seldom will encounter a mugger--and if we did we can't punch him in the nose and expect that he will turn and run before shooting us. Instead, we worry about those things, whether or not they will ever happen is irrelevant, we just worry about them anyway. Unfortunately, our bodies respond to any threat as if the threat is real, immediate and requires an immediate physical response.

So, when a person is embarrassed and feels threatened by what others think, the body triggers the fight-or-flight response, the adrenaline response, and begins preparing for the expected battle. A person experiencing a panic attack is actually experiencing an overreaction of this response system. If you examine the list of symptoms of a panic attack, you see that each of the symptoms of a panic attack is simply some of the normal body responses in the fight-or-flight response.

If we moved into immediate action in response to the perceived threat or attack, our bodies would dissipate these chemicals through physical action, the response would end and our bodies would return to normal.

But, we don't. We respond to the perceived threat or attack with an outpouring into our bloodstream of the appropriate chemicals, but then we don't physically act. The reasons we don't act are varied. Many times the threat is only in our minds, or it is a perceived verbal threat from our boss whom we can't act against, or some other situation where physical action is entirely inappropriate.

Tension in our lives may cause us to do something about these tensions and sometimes that is beneficial. If we hate our job enough we might just go out and get another one. If we have money troubles we might decide to sell our house and move to something smaller. If we worry about muggers and thieves we might move to a smaller town or a safer neighborhood. So this anxiety can be beneficial if it mobilizes us to do something that will make our lives better.

"I'm Afraid to Go to Sleep"

Dottie delayed going to bed night after night. She cleaned the house, read, baked cookies--anything that would delay the terror she had come to expect as she fell asleep. "I could hear a noise like the smoke alarm going off, or a fire engine going past my house, but I knew they were inside my head," she says. "I could feel my teeth grinding and my arms and legs were dead weights. I couldn't move them to try and wake myself up. The rest of my body would be shaking and my heart pounding. There have been times when I believed I had stopped breathing."

While all this is happening, Dottie is aware that she is asleep and in order to make this nightmare go away, she has to wake up.

Dr. Thomas W. Uhde, Chief of the Section of Anxiety and Affective Disorders at the National Institute of Mental Health in Bethesda, MD, says that 60 to 70 percent of panic disorder patients will have at least one severe sleep panic attack in their lifetime, about a third will have recurring sleep panic attacks and 5 percent will have panic attacks more often during sleep than while awake.

What Does a Panic Attack Feel Like?

The "unexpected" aspect of the panic attack is an essential feature. They usually begin with the sudden onset of intense apprehension, fear or terror. Often there is a feeling of impending doom. The symptoms could include: shortness of breath or smothering sensations; dizziness, unsteady feelings, or faintness; choking; palpitations or accelerated heart rate; trembling or shaking; sweating; nausea or abdominal distress; depersonalization or derealization; numbness or tingling sensations; flushes (hot flashes) or chills, chest pain or discomfort; fear of dying; fear of going crazy or of doing something uncontrolled during the attack.

And there is nothing in the present environment to cause such a reaction.

The very first panic attack seems to come completely "out of the blue" and occurs while a person is engaged in some ordinary activity like driving a car or walking to work. Suddenly, the person is struck by a barrage of frightening and uncomfortable symptoms. This barrage of symptoms usually lasts several seconds, but may continue for several minutes. The symptoms gradually fade over the course of about an hour. People who have experienced a panic attack say that it is extremely uncomfortable and that they feared they were being stricken with some terrible, life-threatening disease or were going out of their minds.

Initial panic attacks may occur when people are under considerable stress, from an overload of work or from the loss of a family member or close friend. The attacks may follow surgery, a serious accident, illness or childbirth.

The initial panic attack usually takes the person completely by surprise. This unpredictability is one reason they are so devastating.

People who have never had a panic attack assume that panic is just a matter of feeling nervous or anxious--the sort of feelings that everyone is familiar with. In fact, even though people who have panic attacks may not show any outward signs of discomfort, the feelings they experience are so overwhelming and terrifying that they really believe they are going to die, lose their minds, or be totally humiliated. These disastrous consequences don't occur but they seem quite likely to the person who is suffering a panic attack.

Everett's Life of "Living Hell"

Everett is a handsome young man. Tall, prematurely gray at the temples, he carries himself with confidence but his hands tremble when he pauses to light his cigarette.

"My life is a living hell," he said. "I can't sleep, I can't eat, I don't know what to do next. I have a successful business, I have made a small fortune in real estate but none of that matters if I can't handle worrying about when I am going to go nuts again."

Everett had been showing a large office building to a prospective client. They seemed to have connected with each other from the very beginning. "We were chatting about the usual things you discuss in a commercial property. The parking, what type of clients already had rented space in the building, what the annual occupancy was, that type of thing, when the most awful feeling came over me. The room began to spin, I couldn't keep my balance and I had to lean on the client for support because I was going to faint."

An ambulance took Everett to the nearest hospital. "I never saw the client again and I can understand that--but since then I haven't been able to go into a commercial building. When I try, I have this most horrible feeling that the building isn't real, I begin to tremble and I think I am going to go out of control and smash all the windows or something, just to prove to myself that the building is really there." Everett put out his cigarette and lit another one. "How can I work at a job that requires me to go into commercial buildings if I am unable to do so?"

What Everett was now experiencing was the nervousness and apprehension that developed as the result of his first panic attack. He was now focusing on the fear of having another attack.

This fear--called anticipatory anxiety, or fear of fear--can be present most of the time and seriously interfere with the person's life even when a panic attack is not in progress. In addition, the person may develop irrational fears called phobias about situations where a panic attack has occurred. For example, someone who has had a panic attack while driving may be afraid to get behind the wheel again, even to drive to the grocery store.

People who develop these panic-induced phobias will tend to avoid situations that they fear will trigger a panic attack, and their lives may be increasingly limited as a result. Work may suffer because they can't travel or get to work on time. Relationships may be strained or marred by conflict as panic attacks, or the fear of them, rule the affected persons and those close to them.

Sleep may be disturbed because of panic attacks that occur at night, causing the person to awaken in a state of terror. The experience is so harrowing that some people who have nocturnal panic attacks become afraid to go to sleep and suffer from exhaustion. Also, even if there are no nocturnal panic attacks, sleep may be disturbed because of chronic, panic related anxiety.

Why More Women Than Men?

The statistics indicate that more women worry than men (anxiety among women ranks as the number one psychiatric disorder in all age-groups) and mental health experts are apt to agree. "It's not that men don't ever suffer from anxiety, it's just that they are less likely than women to seek psychiatric help. Instead, they tend to ignore the problem," says Dr. Moreines, "or turn to alcohol to control their panic." Studies at the National Institute of Mental Health show that alcohol abuse is twice as common among men as women, and that as many as one-third to one-half of all alcoholics suffer from phobias or panic disorders.

There is another important difference between men and women: hormones. Anxiety levels may fluctuate with a woman's monthly cycle, notes Dr. Moreines. "Women have a more complex physiology, and something more complex is likely to have built in to it the possibility of problems."

Shirley Swede, coauthor of *The Panic Attack Recovery Book* and founder of the Panic Attack Sufferers' Support Groups, Inc., also thinks the high incidence of anxiety disorders among women is hormone related. "During the progesterone cycle before their periods, women tend to be more nervous and irritable," she says. "Water retention irritates the nervous system, makes you more likely to feel shaky and irritable."

The origins of anxiety and panic also have a cultural component: Little girls are raised to look pretty and be happy, while little boys are told to be assertive and active. When a little girl loses something, for example, her mother might help her find it, while a little boy is often encouraged to find it himself.

"Little girls learn to feel powerless," says Robert Handly, author of *Why Women Worry*. "Boys, on the other hand, learn to approach difficult situations with a more confident, problem solving mentality."

Compound this cultural component for little girls, add the hormonal shifts which take place at puberty, as well as genetic predispositions, and you can easily understand how this can set the stage for anxiety-related disorders.

According to a study conducted by the National Institute of Mental Health, women trying to cope with both family and career are particularly vulnerable.

An Early Start for Panic

Researchers at the Medical University of South Carolina in Charleston state that panic disorder may be more common in school-aged children than it has generally been assumed. Children who display symptoms similar to those associated with adult panic disorder and agoraphobia are usually given a diagnosis specific to childhood, such as separation anxiety. When these researchers treated 3 such children, however, they found that their symptoms met adult criteria for panic disorders.

New York psychiatrist Donna Moreau found that children as young as 7 are subject to panic disorder, which she also felt was often misdiagnosed as school phobia or separation anxiety. Dr. Moreau feels that identifying and treating panic-prone children may stave off serious consequences in adulthood.

The Global Disorder

Heinz Katschnig, of the University of Vienna, reported that an international study shows that panic disorder occurs throughout the world and involves several universal symptoms such as heart palpitation, dizziness, and faintness. Katschnig, who directed a collaborative study that involved interviews of 1,168 panic disorder patients from 14 countries, said that the heart is at the core of panic disorder across cultures. He suggests that any differences in the symptoms of panic disorders may only be due to differences in cultural influences. Michael Amering, of the University of Vienna, also says that the disorder is not limited to Western industrialized countries. He has cited examples of cases in Greenland and Southeast Asia.

Chapter 2
Anxiety Disorders

Aɴxɪᴇᴛʏ ᴀɴᴅ ғᴇᴀʀ ᴀʀᴇ ʙᴏᴛʜ ᴠᴇʀʏ ɴᴏʀᴍᴀʟ ʀᴇsᴘᴏɴsᴇs to a perceived threat. Anxiety is felt when we are expecting something unpleasant is about to happen, and fear occurs when we realize there is a well-defined threat. Both anxiety and fear trigger a sense of helplessness and apprehension, and trigger a vast range of physical symptoms which can range from simply becoming more alert to a pounding heart and uncontrollable trembling.

Individuals with anxiety-related difficulties sometimes feel that they alone suffer from such a problem. The National Institute of Mental Health ranks anxiety disorders as the most common mental health problem in the United States.

The Diagnostic and Statistical Manual of Mental Disorders, the handbook of the American Psychiatric Association, lists a variety of disorders under "Anxiety Disorders." The characteristic features of this group of disorders are symptoms of anxiety and avoidance behaviors.

Generalized Anxiety Disorder

An individual with generalized anxiety disorder has experienced unrealistic or excessive anxiety and worry about two or more life circumstances for six months or longer, during which the person has been bothered more days than not by these concerns. For example, the worry might center on the possibility that it would not be possible to pay the next mortgage while holding down a well paying job, or the concern might be that a child would be unable to attend college while that child is only in elementary school. In a child or adolescent, this may take the form of anxiety and worry about academic, athletic and social performance.

In addition, at least six of the following symptoms are often present when anxious:

Motor Tension
> trembling, twitching, or feeling shaky
> muscle tension, aches, or soreness
> restlessness
> easy fatigability

Autonomic Hyperactivity
> shortness of breath or smothering sensations
> palpitations or accelerated heart rate
> sweating, or cold clammy hands
> dry mouth

dizziness or light-headedness
nausea, diarrhea, or other abdominal distress
flushes (hot flashes) or chills
frequent urination
trouble swallowing or "lump in the throat"

Vigilance and Scanning
feeling keyed up or on edge
exaggerated startle response
difficulty concentrating or "mind going blank"
trouble falling or staying asleep
irritability

Mary's Money Worries

Mary is only thirty-two years old but she is worried most of the time about money. She buys her clothing at second-hand stores and seldom has her hair done profession-ally or takes a vacation. Although she has a well-paying job as a senior librarian at the county library in her hometown, she is con-stantly concerned that there will be cut-backs or that the government might decide to close the library altogether. Mary always worries about unforeseen emergencies--car repairs, dental expenses, things that might deplete her bank account. Mary has more than a year's wages in the bank, only rents a small apartment because she is afraid she would be unable to meet a mortgage payment, and drives a twelve-year-old car. "Because I am single I am aware that there is no one for me to fall back on if I should lose my job."

Mary has a college degree and she has taken a number of computer courses in her spare time so that she might be qualified for some other type of work should the need arise. "I spend a lot of my time obsessing about ways that I might earn extra money-- tutoring, bartending, working in a fast food restaurant.

"At the same time I know that because of the rotating library hours when we are open some evenings and Saturdays, I don't have the capacity to take on another job. I am always aware that I need to put addi- tional money away just in case of some emer- gency. So then I start to think, 'I can't take another job. But I need money!' Then the whole cycle starts over: I need more money. . .I need another job. . .I don't have time for an- other job. . .I need money." Mary's unrealis- tic worrying is a typical example of a generalized anxiety disorder.

Social Phobia

The essential feature of this disorder is a persistent fear of one or more situations in which the person is exposed to possible scrutiny by others and fears that he or she may do something or act in a way that will be humiliating or embarrassing.

The social phobic fear may be circumscribed, such as fears of being unable to continue talking while speaking in public, choking on food when eating in front of others, being unable to urinate in a public lavatory, or having a hand tremble when writing in the presence of others. In other cases the social phobic fears may involve most social situations, such as general fears of saying foolish things or not being able to answer questions in social situations.

During some phase of the disturbance, exposure to the specific phobic stimulus almost invariably provokes an immediate anxiety response. Thus, for example, someone who fears speaking in public, when forced to do so, will almost invariably have an immediate anxiety response, such as feeling panicky, sweating, experiencing a racing heart and difficulty breathing.

Anticipatory anxiety occurs when the person is confronted with the necessity of entering into the phobic situation, and such situations are most often avoided. Occasionally, the individual will force himself or herself to endure the social phobic situation and then experience intense anxiety. The individual then will fear that others will detect the signs of anxiety that the social phobic situation arouses and a vicious cycle may be created in which this fear generates anxiety that impairs performance, thus increasing the motivation to avoid the situation.

The social phobic is most often afraid of: blushing, humiliation, job interviews, using public toilets, crowds and parties. It is easy to see that the socially phobic individual who must occasionally be required to perform in public might use alcohol, tranquilizers or some other types of medication in order to "appear" calm or "to calm the nerves" to meet this phobic situation, when required to do so by peer pressure, occupational or academic necessity.

Sam's Social Situation

Sam works in a large bank on the main floor of a twenty-six floor office building. Well-liked by his colleagues and quick to joke with others at coffee time, Sam appears to be easy-going and calm.

"What people don't know about me," says Sam "is that I am often feeling 'quaky' inside. If I drink just one cup of coffee at break time the feeling begins. At first it is sort of pleasant, I have an edge of alertness, but then my hands begin to tremble and I often put them in my pockets so no one will see them."

Sam's difficulties began when the building decided that it needed increased security at the entrance to the building. "It was decided that everyone had to sign-in every time they entered. Management put a big burly security guard behind a desk right at the front door. Even though he saw you every day and got to know the regular employees, you had to sign in on a log book in front of him.

"I couldn't do it," Sam said. "My hand would shake so badly that I had to control it with the other hand in order to hit the line and then you couldn't read what I had written. I know he thought I was nuts and a suspicious character, someone who had something to hide. He probably thought I had a drinking problem and had a hangover with the 'shakes' every morning." Sam began to stay in at lunch so he only had to deal with the problem once a day. "I practiced at home at night, shortening my signature so that it was just kind of a slash with a capital letter at the beginning. I would wake up in the middle of the night worrying about how I was going to get into the building in the morning."

Eventually the guard reported Sam to management as someone "suspicious," and Sam found himself in the office of the bank vice president, trying to explain his fear of writing his own name while someone watched him. Fortunately, Sam's boss was understanding, listened to Sam and believed him about his anxiety about writing.

"I guess he had a hard time believing that I was plotting to rob the bank," Sam laughed, "but at the same time he thought it was really a handicap for me. He suggested that I see a therapist before someone else thought my behavior was suspicious." Sam got help for this social phobia and was able to keep his job.

Obsessive-Compulsive Disorder

The essential feature of this disorder is recurrent obsessions or compulsions sufficiently severe to cause marked distress, be time-consuming, or significantly interfere with the person's normal routine, occupational functioning, or usual social activities or relationships with others.

Obsessions are persistent ideas, thoughts, impulses, or images that are experienced, at least initially, as intrusive and senseless--for example, thoughts of violence to a loved pet. The person attempts to ignore or suppress such thoughts or impulses or to neutralize them with some other thought or action. The sufferer recognizes that the obsessions are the product or his or her own mind, and are not imposed from without (as in the delusional individual who hears voices which he or she believes are speaking to him from some other place).

The most common obsessions are repetitive thoughts of violence (killing one's child or parent), contamination (becoming infected by shaking hands), and doubt (repeatedly wondering whether one has performed some act, such as having hurt someone).

Compulsions are repetitive, purposeful, and intentional behaviors that are performed in response to an obsession, according to certain rules, or in a stereotyped fashion.

The behavior is designed to neutralize, or prevent discomfort in, some dreaded event or situation. However, either the activity is not connected in a realistic way with what it is designed to neutralize or prevent, or it is clearly excessive. The act is performed with a sense of subjective compulsion that is coupled with a desire to resist the compulsion. The person recognizes that his or her behavior is excessive or unreasonable and does not derive pleasure from carrying out the activity, although it provides a release of tension. The most common compulsions involve hand-washing, counting, checking, and touching.

When the person attempts to resist a compulsion, there is a sense of mounting tension that can be immediately relieved by yielding to the compulsion. After repeated failure at resisting the compulsions, the person may give in to them and no longer experience a desire to resist.

Depression and anxiety are common. Frequently there is a phobic avoidance of situations that involve the content of the obsessions, such as dirt or contamination. For example, a person with obsessions about dirt may avoid public rest rooms, a person with obsessions about contamination may avoid shaking hands with strangers.

The obsessions or compulsions cause marked distress, are time-consuming (take more than an hour a day), or significantly interfere with the person's normal routine, occupational functioning, or usual social activities or relationships with others.

Studies have shown that obsessive-compulsive disorder affects approximately 2 percent of the population. It is equally common among both men and women; it is more common among those who are young, divorced or separated, and is less common among black or Hispanics.

It is increasingly clear that obsessive-compulsive disorder is caused by an abnormal pattern of energy flow in the caudate nucleus, the part of the human brain corresponding to the section of the animal brain which controls instinctive, repetitive behavior such as grooming and nesting.

Florence's Compulsion

Florence is an ordinary-looking middle-aged woman who usually dressed for comfort. She raised four children in a nice home and when the last child went off to school, for the first time found herself without anyone at home during the day. Frequently she went out and met other women to have lunch or play bridge or for a day of shopping.

Florence began to worry every time she left the house that she had either left the iron or the stove turned on and as a result of her carelessness the house might catch fire and burn down. At first she would go back and check once and reassure herself that she had turned her appliances off. After a while, she found that even though she did that, she would get no more than a block from her house when she would be compelled to go back and check again.

Sometimes Florence would have to leave in the middle of a bridge game or lunch to be absolutely certain that she had turned them off, even though she knew she had already checked a dozen times before.

Ashamed of this compulsion, she told no one, not even her husband of many years. She got creative with excuses to explain why she had to go home.

When Florence found she could no longer leave her house without physical manifestations of her fears, she began to stay home so that she could check on her appliances as often as she wanted during the day. Florence was now completely controlled by her compulsion. Ultimately, Florence's husband rebelled when she would no longer go out to dinner or any other function with him, making feeble excuses that no longer held up. Both were amazed to find that there was a treatment for this disorder, and within six months Florence was able to control her ritual behavior by approximately 80 percent. She is working hard to become completely free of the disorder.

Post-Traumatic Stress Disorder

Following a psychologically distressing event that is outside the range of usual human experience such as rape, assault, a natural disaster such as an earthquake, major surgery, combat duty during war, or being in a serious accident or witnessing such an event, can cause post-traumatic stress disorder. The incident which causes this disorder would be extremely distressing to anyone, and is usually experienced with intense fear, terror, and a feeling of helplessness.

The most common traumatic events involve either a serious threat to one's life or physical integrity; a serious threat or harm to one's children, spouse, or other close relatives or friends; sudden destruction of one's home or community; or seeing another person seriously injured or killed as a result of an accident or physical violence.

Some stressors frequently produce the disorder (torture is an example) and others produce it only occasionally (natural disasters or auto accidents).

A person experiencing post-traumatic stress disorder will often re-experience the traumatic event--known by war veterans as "flashbacks." Ironically, it is when life calms down and things seem to be going well, that is when the unconscious begins to open up, causing the flashbacks and breakthroughs of these repressed memories. The sufferer will avoid any stimuli associated with the event or will experience a numbing of general responsiveness, and increased arousal, such as a startle reflex at unexpected sounds, such as a car backfiring.

The event can be re-experienced in a variety of ways. Often recurrent and intrusive recollections or recurrent distressing dreams occur. There is often intense psychological distress when the person is exposed to events that resemble an aspect of the event or symbolize the event, such as anniversaries.

Decreased responsiveness to the external world, referred to as "psychic numbing" or "emotional anesthesia," will begin soon after the original experience. A person may complain of feeling detached or estranged from others, that he or she has lost the ability to become interested in previously enjoyed activities, or that the ability to feel emotions of any type, particularly those associated with intimacy, tenderness, and sexuality, is decreased. Police officers often find that they can no longer relate to their families after witnessing violent death scenes or chasing an armed suspect down a dark street. They often find their lives torn by divorce, with their spouse complaining that they are distant and non-caring.

Individuals may find that they have difficulty in falling asleep or staying asleep. There may be a lack of ability to concentrate or complete tasks. They become hyper-vigilant. Attention is riveted on the external world, scanning for the next danger or attack, either real or imagined. Senses are hyper-alert. The immune and digestive systems are depressed, and as the body's supply of energy is used up, stress and fatigue set in. Individuals with post-traumatic stress disorder run on pure adrenaline.

Many war veterans report they feel guilty and responsible for a buddy who was killed or for violent acts they had to perform as part of their military activities.

For those who have actually committed acts of violence, the fear is conscious and individuals may worry increasingly about their ability to control aggression and rage.

This continuous stress causes chemical changes in the body and the brain. The neurotransmitters become inoperable or inefficient and the natural opiates for fighting pain and stress become overtaxed. The inability to concentrate often results in forgetfulness. There may be a craving for food, drugs or alcohol, resulting in addictions.

The symptoms can be intensified when the person is exposed to situations or activities that resemble or symbolize the original trauma (the sound of a helicopter overhead, a fog shrouded highway).

Some people develop a chaotic life-style as a defense against these internal conflicts. In order to avoid the internal pain, they project it onto the environment by creating crises. Traveling from crisis to crisis, they keep their attention focused on the immediate emergency.

When someone is changed by a traumatic incident, there is a sense of loss of self. Often the person begins to run on raw adrenaline and turns to alcohol or drugs to dampen down the symptoms. The more self-medication, the more ineffective it becomes. Ultimately, a deep depression sets in. Upon recovery, it may take up to two years for the neurotransmitters to heal and this may cause hyper-alertness to continue, even though the person is making progress in healing.

Post-traumatic stress disorder requires the assistance of a therapist to learn to accept what happened, integrate it, forgive the trauma, pain and anger; as well as all the other life-style changes that the other anxiety disorders require, such as diet, sleep, exercise, meditation and help to develop coping skills.

The Trauma of Lenore

Lenore is an eight-year-old child of the inner city. She is never allowed outside to play in the street and her mother walks her back and forth to school daily. Nevertheless, Lenore experienced a drive-by shooting. She saw several teenagers she knew die violently as she stood in the school yard waiting for her mother to come and get her on a beautiful autumn day.

Lenore, who had been a good and conscientious student up until that time, found that she had difficulty concentrating, frequent headaches, and began to make excuses to stay home from school after the incident.

Lenore had almost quit talking; she became silent and unresponsive in class and, while well behaved, she is no longer one of the leaders of her group.

When questioned, Lenore very reluctantly told her mother that she spends a lot of time thinking about what she must do to survive if she sees cars speeding past her; that she wakes up in a panic anytime she hears tires squealing on the pavement outside her window at night; and she doesn't think that she should make any plans for her future because she might not be alive at this same time next year. She has spent a lot of time wondering if she could have done anything to save the victims or if she should have been able to give a description of the shooter to the police.

With the assistance of a therapist who had worked with many victims of violent crime, Lenore began to accept what she witnessed. Slowly the therapist was able to make her realize that there was absolutely nothing that she could have done to change what had happened. Lenore was encouraged to make plans for her own safety and she is slowly beginning to let go of the trauma.

Simple Phobia

Few of us like to see a spider crawling down the wall. And most of us clench our teeth and start to sweat a little when an airplane ride turns bumpy. But what if those natural fears become so intense that normal life becomes difficult or impossible? What if we fled in panic at the sight of any insect or refused to board an airplane, no matter what?

Then our fear has crossed the line into phobia, says Anne Marie Albano, assistant director of the Center for Stress and Anxiety Disorders at the State University of New York at Albany. "Unrealistic fear that is all out of proportion to the actual threat is a phobia."

The most common fears people have are of animals or insects, natural elements like storms and water, and heights or closed-in spaces, like elevators. One traumatic event may trigger the phobia. An assault by one dog, for example, may lead to a fear of all dogs. "If someone comes to the center with a phobia, we often find that another member of the family has a phobia too," says Dr. Albano.

A person who is afraid of mice will have an immediate anxiety response upon seeing one. They might feel panicky, sweaty, have a pounding heart and difficulty breathing. The knowledge that the individual is terrified of mice will often result in avoidance of places where mice might be encountered such as basements or pet shops.

Someone who is afraid of flying does not experience that fear except when required to get onto a plane. An individual who fears snakes simply avoids them.

Simple phobias are quite common and do not usually create major problems unless the feared object or situation cannot easily be avoided. Some of the more common phobias are the persistent fear of objects or situations such as snakes, dogs, flying, elevators, heights, bridges. The anxiety is focused on a specific external object or situation and is only present when that specific object or situation is encountered.

However, phobias can spread if the original phobia isn't strong enough to contain all the person's fear and anxiety. Every time you panic from your phobia, a brand new phobia might spring up. If you fear elevators, you might suddenly find yourself with a new phobia to snakes or thunder or almost anything else you can think of.

Another way phobias spread is to generalize. Someone who is afraid of scissors, for example, may generalize that not only scissors, but all things that cut or have sharp edges are dangerous, and go on to include things such as knives or various tools.

Leslie and Harry Rise to the Occasion

Leslie is not sure just when he began to fear elevators but he realized that when he got on one and the door started to close, his anxiety level would rise and he would have difficulty breathing. While his heart pounded and his palms got sweaty, he would try to keep any other passengers on the elevator from realizing that anything was wrong and, of course, that just increased his anxiety level. After a while his anxiety got so severe that he would have to get off the elevator several floors before his destination and take the stairs the rest of the way.

Leslie finally decided just to avoid elevators. He often jokes about it: "I'm terrified of elevators (I met my wife on one)--but I need the exercise." Leaving co-workers, he races to the stairs and is frequently there to greet them when they get off at their floor.

Leslie's wife of eighteen years isn't upset by his joke. "If that's what it takes, I don't care, everybody knows Leslie is a character."

Says Leslie, "I don't hide it, everyone is afraid of something. I just happen to be afraid of elevators. I guess if it was absolutely something I had to do, like driving to work, then I would be forced to do something about it--but meanwhile, I just laugh and run up the stairs."

Harry had a similar phobia--fear of elevators. But Harry wasn't as lucky as Leslie. Try as he might, he was unable to contain his elevator phobia and just like Leslie, he began to take the stairs. One day, as he entered the stairwell for the trip up seven flights to his office, he panicked at the sight of the handrail! Harry's phobia had spread. That day, he was unable to go to work because there was absolutely no way he could get there. Harry says, "I couldn't get on the elevator, I couldn't get on the stairs--the only thing I could have done was climb up the outside of the building. I was more willing to do that than I was to do either of the other options! I had no choice, I had to get some help to combat my phobias."

Harry was fortunate. His Employee Assistance Program immediately put him in touch with a therapist who specialized in phobias and he was soon on his way to recovery.

Harry, who heard Leslie's story, says, "Maybe his phobia won't generalize and he will be able to run up the stairs for the rest of his life but maybe he won't either. I think he should get help and stop making a joke about it. Phobias are no laughing matter, even though others who don't have them think they are."

Panic Disorder

The main feature of panic disorder is that the panic occurs completely "out of the blue," for no apparent reason. No threat is present nor does it seem that you have any medical condition that would cause you to become dizzy, unable to breathe, or any of the other physical manifestations of extreme terror. Sometimes you will experience feelings of impending doom, while you hear a loud buzzing in your ears. Your skin is tingling and your legs feel like mush.

Individuals who experience panic attacks usually do not avoid places or situations that they associate with panic. After only one experience with panic attacks however, many people focus on the possibility of having another attack. This is known as "anticipatory anxiety." Now the worry begins, "What if this happens again?" The worry and fear continue, "I hope it won't happen again." The worry and fear increase; "What if it happens in a meeting, or while I'm driving, or what-if, what-if, what-if." And now the round of doctor and emergency room visits begin, all the while keeping the panic a secret while you worry, worry, worry.

Sandra--A Casualty of Panic

Sandra, who had her first full-blown panic attack on the commuter train, soon found that the horrible experience was not an isolated incident. After the experience on the train she had more attacks until, after approximately eight months, she was having one or more panic attacks a day. Sandra then became a victim of the emergency room experience--she was told that there was nothing wrong with her, one doctor even went as far as to tell her to "stop being a hysterical female."

Despite being told there was nothing wrong, Sandra was convinced that she was soon going to die. She quit her job and went home to live with her parents. She soon discovered that if she stayed at home where she was comfortable, her panic attacks decreased. She began avoiding going out and became completely housebound. Now Sandra had Panic disorder with Agoraphobia.

Panic with Agoraphobia

Panic disorder may progress to this more advanced stage form of the disorder. In addition to suffering from panic attacks and all the excruciating symptoms that accompany them, you (the agoraphobic) fear being in places or situations where escape might not be possible or someplace where you might be embarrassed should you have a panic attack.

As the result of this fear, you begin to either restrict your travel or find that you must have a support person accompany you if you do go out.

Typically, people with agoraphobia fear being in crowds, standing in line, entering shopping malls, and riding in cars or public transportation. This avoidance can range from mild to severe. For some individuals, there might be a 'safe' distance they can travel--perhaps two or three miles from home. Even when they restrict themselves to "safe" situations, most people with agoraphobia continue to have panic attacks at least a few times a month.

People with agoraphobia can be seriously disabled by their condition. Severe agoraphobia often limits sufferers to their homes, sometimes for years at a time. Some are unable to work and need to rely heavily on other family members. Agoraphobics must allow their support person (often a spouse or parent) to do all the errands, and rely on them totally for emotional support.

Thus the person with agoraphobia typically leads a life of extreme dependency as well as great discomfort. The result of such demands ultimately affects not only the sufferer but family members as well; it can prevent the support person from having any life of their own and eventually it can destroy the relationship.

Agoraphobia affects about a third of all people with panic disorder. Psychiatrist Alan Breier, of the National Institute of Mental Health, and colleagues studied the relationship between agoraphobia and panic attacks in individuals suffering from either or both disorders. They found that patients with both disorders almost always had the panic attack first. In about 75 percent of the cases, agoraphobic episodes began within a year of the initial panic attack. The researchers believe that the agoraphobia may have been brought on by the patient's fear of suffering a panic attack in a public place.

Sandra's Ultimate Solution

Despite pleas from both of her parents, Sandra refused to confront her problem, finding it easier to complain that they "just couldn't understand." She continued to stay home and rely totally on her mother, who appeared to enjoy having Sandra at home and encouraged the dependent relationship, despite the problems it caused in her relationship with Sandra's father.

After four years, Sandra's mother died. Sandra found that, although her father tried to be sympathetic, he was unable and unwilling to be with her all the time.

While her father was at work Sandra often filled her days lying on the couch and watching television. One day she just happened to see a local television news program on panic disorder, featuring a local therapist. "Suddenly, it was all clear to me. I wasn't going to die, I wasn't insane. Whatever was wrong with me, it sounded like here was finally someone who understood. She certainly was describing my life and my symptoms." Sandra called the news station and got the telephone number of the therapist, who specialized in panic disorder. "I want to be able to go out of the house just like everybody else. I want to get my independence back," Sandra told her. She had taken that first step on the road to recovery.

Chapter 3
Is It "Nerves" or Something Else?

THERE ARE A MULTITUDE OF PHYSICAL and, as we have just seen, psychiatric conditions, which have some of the same symptoms of anxiety and its extreme--panic. For this very reason, it makes sense if you are experiencing such symptoms to have a thorough medical examination and laboratory work-up before deciding for yourself just what these symptoms mean and what is wrong.

An erroneous self-diagnosis of heart attack or mental illness is easy to make. If you do that, you may spend years being either a "heart cripple" or a "crazy person" and still never really know what is wrong with you. Your symptoms and your worries about them just continue--sometimes for years. It is best to have an examination for a proper diagnosis.

A study at Harvard's Massachusetts General Hospital found that 70 percent of panic attack patients had been to more than ten physicians each before they were properly diagnosed. Those who seek treatment for panic attacks are more likely to visit family doctors, internists, gynecologists, cardiologists and other non-psychiatric physicians than to see mental health professionals.

After listening to the insomnia, exhaustion, head-aches, upset stomachs and other physical ailments that accompany an anxiety disorder--after ruling out the obvious possible physical causes for the patient's symptoms--these physicians often diagnose the patient as being a hypochondriac or just anxious. Sometimes these doctors just listen to the symptoms and "decide," without any blood tests or anything more elaborate than a visual inspection and a cursory listen to the heart and lungs with a stethoscope, that the patient was suffering from simply being neurotic.

This type of diagnosis is one of the reasons why it is absolutely necessary to insist on a thorough medical examination and laboratory work-up before accepting any diagnosis.

After a series of such superficial diagnoses, it is easy to understand why someone might just give up and accept their own diagnosis. One of the difficulties anxiety-prone people face is that they can allow their own feelings of helplessness and lack of control over their suffering to prevent them from seeking treatment--either initially or after a series of misdiagnoses. Don't just decide that you are "anxiety-prone" or that "everybody in my family is high-strung" and go on suffering because it seems to be the only way to live. It isn't. Get a proper diagnosis first, which must include both a complete physical and thorough laboratory work-up, and then be in a position to make an intelligent decision about what to do next.

Panic Attack

The American Psychiatric Association's criteria for diagnosing any patient is outlined in their manual, *The Diagnostic and Statistical Manual of Mental Disorders*, known as DSM-III-R. This book lists mental disorders and their symptoms.

Criteria for panic attack:

A. At some time during the disturbance, one or more panic attacks (discrete periods of intense fear or discomfort) have occurred that were (1) unexpected, i.e., did not occur immediately before or on exposure to a situation that almost always caused anxiety, and (2) not triggered by situations in which the person was the focus of other's attention.

B. Either four attacks, as described in criterion A, have occurred within a four week period, or one or more attacks have been followed by a period of at least a month of persistent fear of having another attack.

C. At least four of the following symptoms developed during at least one of the attacks:

(1) shortness of breath or smothering sensations

(2) dizziness, unsteady feelings, or faintness

(3) palpitations or accelerated heart rate

(4) trembling or shaking

(5) sweating

(6) choking

(7) nausea or abdominal stress

(8) depersonalization or derealization

(9) numbness or tingling sensations

(10) flushes or chills

(11) chest pain or discomfort

(12) fear of dying

(13) fear of going crazy or doing something uncontrolled

NOTE: Attacks involving four or more symptoms are panic attacks; attacks involving fewer than four symptoms are limited symptom attacks.

D. During at least some of the attacks, at least four of the "C" symptoms developed suddenly and increased in intensity within ten minutes of the beginning of the first "C" symptom noticed in the attack.

E. It cannot be established that an organic factor

initiated and maintained the disturbance, e.g., amphetamine or caffeine intoxication, or hyperthyroidism.

Note: Mitral valve prolapse may be an associated condition, but does not preclude a diagnosis of Panic Disorder.

Reprinted by permission from: *The Diagnostic and Statistical Manual of Mental Disorders*, Third Edition, Revised, American Psychiatric Association, Washington, D.C. 1987.

This is quite a lengthy description of symptoms and anyone who has ever experienced a panic attack probably recognizes most of them.

But before you say, "Ah! I must have panic attacks," read the following list of medical conditions which could also have some similar symptoms.

It is quite possible that you could have some undiagnosed medical condition, which ought to be treated first. These are just some of the possible ailments that should be considered before making a diagnosis of an anxiety or panic disorder.

Endocrine System Disorders

"That Stressed-Out Feeling Never Stopped"

Alice couldn't sleep and she found herself making more and more mistakes at work. Her supervisor Fred, who had always thought highly of Alice, and had always found her to be an exemplary employee, spoke gently to her about these errors at first,

"I was very ashamed. I apologized profusely and lectured myself to pay more attention, although I was exhausted in the morning because of my insomnia. I couldn't tell Fred I wasn't sleeping because I knew he would ask me questions about what was going on in my personal life. I thought he probably would send me to Employee Assistance through our Personnel Department, a program for people with 'emotional or drug' problems."

But Alice continued to make errors and found herself in trouble, with the possibility of actually losing her job a reality.

"I never really considered that I could lose my job. Fred was no longer so sympathetic. In fact, he was quite harsh and told me he was going to put me on probation. I was absolutely horrified and in a continual state of anxiety after that meeting."

Alice began to lose weight and worried continuously about making more mistakes. "First of all, I couldn't believe that I was being threatened with probation. I considered myself a conscientious worker and sort of a workaholic. I am always the first there in the morning and the last to leave at night. I try to be perfect and in control of the work I have to do.

"Then others began to notice my weight loss and people began to ask questions. I told them I was dieting. I realized they were talking about me, wondering what was wrong. I heard a rumor that I had cancer and all the time I was thinking that I was going crazy."

The next time Alice made a serious error, Fred called her into his office.

"Before he could say anything to me I began to tremble all over. I shook so badly you could see it across the room. I was covered in perspiration. I could no longer pretend that nothing was wrong. I thought I was going to come apart at the seams. Fred got so scared by the way I looked that he called 911 and I went to the hospital in an ambulance."

For Alice this emergency resulted in a diagnosis and treatment. She had hyper-thyroidism.

Hyperthyroidism

An excessively over-productive thyroid gland is one of the most common disorders of the endocrine system and it can easily be misdiagnosed as an anxiety disorder.

This gland delivers thyroid hormone to the body which causes the metabolic rate to rise. When this happens some of the symptoms are hyperactivity, a shortened attention span, insomnia and weight loss.

Excessive sweating, fatigue, heart palpitations and muscular weakness are also very common. Any slight anxiety-producing occurrence will increase these symptoms, and someone who jumps at an unexpected noise and then finds oneself sweating with a pounding heart may very well think that this is panic.

Also, when this type of reaction occurs with any slight insult to the nervous system, the thinking becomes cyclical--with more thyroid hormone produced and more over reaction.

Fearful and Out of Control

Carla was very concerned about her weight. She set herself a limit of 5 pounds increase. If her weight went 5 pounds above her 115 rule, she would diet strenuously. Her usual breakfast was just black coffee but when she was dieting she would drink

themselves in the hands of police because they have been found trembling, confused, and responding to any questioning with slurred speech. It is easy to understand that anyone observing such behavior might mistake it for drunkenness. It is also easy to see that the agitated behavior and disorientation that can occur could also easily be taken as indications of an anxiety attack.

If you have ever felt shaky after missing a meal you know what the beginning of hypoglycemia can feel like.

Hypoglycemia often results when diabetics use too much insulin, but it can also be the result of insulin-secreting tumors of the pancreas. In some cases, early mild diabetes (and studies indicate that over fifty percent of Americans can be considered pre-diabetic: that is, they are at the very edge of having insufficient insulin producing capacity to handle the daily "sugar load" of their dietary intake) can cause a "reactive" hypoglycemia which can occur just hours after a high carbohydrate meal.

Diabetes Mellitus

This condition produces hyperglycemia, just the opposite of hypoglycemia, because the pancreas produces too little insulin to oxidize the carbohydrates eaten.

In addition to the low production of insulin, stress can affect the glucose regulation of the diabetic. Now there is a double insult to the body--too little insulin already being produced and the additional drop in insulin production created by stress.

The high glucose levels of the diabetic and the anxiety level this creates produce symptoms which are similar to those observed by psychiatric patients who suffer from severe anxiety.

Clinical studies have indicated that generalized anxiety disorders are six times more prevalent in diabetics than in non-diabetics.

Cushing's Syndrome

Hyperadrenalism, an overproduction of the hormone ACTH (adrenocorticotrophic hormone), is caused by either hyperactivity of the adrenal glands or by tumors elsewhere in the body which also produce ACTH.

The majority of people with Cushing's Syndrome experience behavioral changes. Depression is the most common one, but it can also trigger anxiety.

Pheochromocytoma

Very small tumors of the medulla secrete excessive levels of catecholamines which are responsible for disturbing the hormonal balance of the body.

Someone with this disorder will have episodes

of severe anxiety, extreme headaches, shortness of breath, heart palpitations and dizziness.

Carcinoid Syndrome

These tumors affect the endocrine cells in the small intestine, stomach or the appendix by some secretions they produce which apparently raise the level of endocrine hormones. About half of patients with these tumors will experience increased levels of anxiety as the result of these secretions.

Panhypopituitarism

The anterior pituitary gland can cease to produce the hormones for which it is responsible as the result of tumors, injury, radiation or infectious disease. A decrease in a number of hormones leads to this condition.

About three-fourths of individuals experience emotional symptoms which include depression and anxiety. Secondary effects are hypoglycemia, hypothyroidism, and hypoten-sion, all of which relate to increased anxiety reaction to stress.

These are all disorders of the **endocrine system**--the thyroid, the parathyroid, the thymus, the hypothalamus and the pituitary, the ovaries and the testes, and the adrenals--a system which is responsible for the production a great number of hormones.

These hormones work to keep the body in balance, acting chemically on body organs to keep growth, blood pressure, heart rate, appetite, sexual drive and other essential bodily processes running correctly.

The little hypothalamus acts as a master gland, regulating all the body's processes from the sleep-wake cycle to heart rate, appetite and emotional response. When this gland senses something is out of balance, it sends instructions to the appropriate gland to either secrete more or less of the needed hormone to keep the body in balance.

The difficulties with endocrine secretions come about when a particular gland fails to produce the proper amount of its hormone. When too much or too little is secreted and an imbalance occurs, the brain becomes aware of this immediately and behavior can change radically as a result, long before the disorder progresses to include easily visible physical symptoms.

The effects of the endocrine system on our mind are very important when it comes to how we think, but often these effects are not diagnosed as being caused by anything physical. Usually nothing visibly indicates there is a hormonal problem, such as bleeding or swelling, and so the symptoms are often given a psychiatric diagnosis. Not only are physicians guilty of such misdiagnosis, the patient often thinks there

is something wrong with her mind long before anyone begins to suspect something so subtle as a hormone imbalance.

The laboratory tests that can detect such endocrine disorders are quite complex and sophisticated.
It is usually not until some physical symptoms are
evident, such as the moon face of Cushing's or the
weight loss of hyperthyroidism, that the physician
and the patient begin to realize that these symptoms
of anxiety may have a physical cause.

Premenstrual Syndrome--A Combination

More than 5.5 million women in the United States
suffer with Premenstrual Syndrome. It is the name
given to a set of symptoms that consistently appear
before or during early menstruation--but which are
absent during the rest of the woman's monthly cycle.
There are more than 150 symptoms of PMS which
can range from mildly annoying to debilitating. Mood
swings are the most common symptom--more than
half of all women experience them. PMS is a progesterone response disorder. It is not a deficiency of the
female sex hormone, rather it is an inhibition of the
body's progesterone receptors. Progesterone receptors are found in large concentration in the brain's
limbic area--known as the "area of rage and violence." Impaired uptake of progesterone in this area

seems to account for the emotional symptoms of PMS, including tension and violent outbursts.

Dr. David T. George and colleagues at the National Institute on Alcohol Abuse and Alcoholism in Bethesda, Maryland, describe the cases of three women who were normally subject to panic attacks but whose panic symptoms showed marked improvement during pregnancy.

The researchers suggest that pregnancy may blunt the activity of the sympathetic nervous system, which speeds up the heartbeat and secretes adrenaline during panic attacks. Hormonal changes associated with pregnancy, as well as the sense of purpose and self-esteem that pregnancy fosters, may also play a role.

Is this suggesting that pregnancy is the answer to panic attacks? Of course not, but what it does point to is the role that hormone levels play in the triggering of panic.

"I Have a Gun and PMS"

PMS is a joke to a lot of people. There are bumper stickers and desk signs warning people that the driver or the occupant of the office is going to excuse their behavior based on "having PMS."

Earl would frequently complain about what he considered the inexplicable behavior of his wife, Holly. He would shrug his shoulders, roll his eyes and say, "She has PMS." That seemed to explain everything.

He would often tell his buddies that she was tense, depressed, irritable, dizzy, given to crying jags and panic attacks--and too tired and cranky to be any fun anymore. Earl thought that her weight gain, migraine headaches and backaches were just "excuses" to avoid sex. Their marriage was headed for serious trouble.

"I had taken Prozac for my symptoms, but I found that I couldn't handle the side effects, so I had to give it up. I didn't want to behave so erratically, but it just seemed that I couldn't control myself. I yelled at Earl, I yelled at the kids, and I have stomped out of all the stores in town when they didn't wait on me quickly enough or have what I wanted to buy."

Earl and Holly were on a fast track to divorce.

Fortunately, Holly read about Katharina Dalton, a gynecological endocrinologist who headed the world's first PMS clinic in London, and was able to get treatment for this common hormonal problem.

"I couldn't believe that anything as simple as a diet could make all the difference in my symptoms but I am here to tell you that it did."

Diseases of the Central Nervous System

Epilepsy

There are a variety of different types of epilepsy-- a disorder where the brain's normal electrical rhythms are interrupted by random bursts of electricity which scramble the brain function.

The obvious seizure, the kind where the patient falls to the floor in convulsions with loss of motor control, is the kind we usually think of when we use the term epilepsy.

Temporal lobe and psychomotor epilepsy are two of the other less well known types which are most likely to produce psychiatric symptoms which could be translated into anxiety or panic. Patients may just pause for a few moments in their daily activities; may appear to be distracted or non-responsive when spoken to.

Between these seizures, the individual may have personality changes, such as anxiety, depression, hysteria and panic, which are brought about by the change in the electrical rhythm in the brain.

Lois' Panic in the Pantry

Lois liked her work in the bakery. She loved the smell of bread baking, the warm loaves on the big silvery trays that she slid onto the shelves early in the morning.

Sometimes Lois would suddenly find herself standing in the middle of the floor and realize that the baker was talking to her. "Lois, why are you just standing there, we need to put more flour into the mix. Quick, quick." When she heard that, Lois would realize she had been on a "mental walkabout," as she called these lapses of her mind and she would quicken her step to get on with her work.

Sometimes after one of her "walkabouts," she would find herself crying and shaking, with legs so weak they would hardly hold her up. She would get very busy with some job that would let her sit down for a while and try to hide her face so no one would see.

Lois's friend Jennifer began to gently talk to her about what was happening. Jennifer said, "You don't seem to be yourself these days, Lois. What's wrong?"

"Oh, nothing," she would always respond, but Lois worried too. She realized that these "walk-abouts" were happening more and more often. The more she worried about them the more they seemed to happen.

Her anxiety level increased and she got herself into "a real state," as she finally told her doctor. The doctor appointment had been difficult for her to make but Jennifer had finally convinced her that something was seriously wrong. Lois had become more and more depressed, more and more panicky and knew it was becoming apparent to everyone at work. Although she was unhappy to hear the diagnosis of psychomotor epilepsy, she was relieved to find she wasn't losing her mind and her "mental walkabouts" could be controlled with medication.

Post-Concussion Syndrome

A severe head injury, where the brain is literally bounced around within the skull cavity, can result in injury to various brain structures, which then results in damage to the temporal lobe. Anxiety, mood swings, personality changes and depression can all be caused by such a head injury which may not have any visible wound, other than a "bump" on the head at the time of the occurrence.

Multiple Sclerosis

This chronic, degenerative neurological disease attacks the sheaths that protect the nerves. In the early stages, before any diagnosis is made, the individual may experience some tingling in the arms and legs, visual disturbances and some temporary weakness in the extremities. Sometimes the patients may feel that they just need to sit down because their legs won't support them. The next day they will feel just fine. Because MS has periods of remission, it is often years before the physical symptoms are sufficient to take the individual to the doctor for a true diagnosis.

When MS affects the frontal and temporal lobes of the brain, it can result in bizarre behavior, which can include feelings of euphoria, depression and anxiety.

These **diseases of the central nervous system** (the brain and the spinal cord) are among the most common copycats of psychiatric disorders. Almost every central nervous system disorder will have some impact on thoughts, emotions, memory and sensation.

Infectious Diseases

Infectious Mononucleosis

A virus which causes this acute infectious disease attacks the disease-fighting white blood cells of the body. It has a sudden onset with fever and inflammatory swelling of the lymph nodes. The physical symptoms include a feeling of extreme fatigue, headaches and sometimes a persistent weakness which can last for weeks after recovery.

The result of this infection can be a chronic feeling of anxiety and fatigue, followed by depression which may no longer be associated with the few weeks of the infection.

Infectious Hepatitis

A viral infection of the liver, this is one of the most common infections in the world. Hepatitis A is caused by contaminated food or water and Hepatitis B through blood transmission. It is possible to become infected by contaminated needles or sexual contact with an infected individual.

During the course of the illness, it is possible to have a variety of psychiatric symptoms along with the medical ones. These can include a mild feeling of lethargy or even include delusions, which can range from anxiety to complete psychosis. After this lengthy illness it is not unusual for sufferers to experience depression which, if unresolved, can evolve into continuing psychiatric difficulties.

Encephalitis

This is an inflammation of the brain that results

from a virus injected into the blood stream through the bite of a mosquito. The symptoms can include headache, nausea, muscle aches, vomiting and visual disturbances. The result of these symptoms may be anxiety which can progress to prolonged anxiety symptoms.

These are just some of the **infectious diseases** that can result in psychiatric disorders.

Metabolic Disorders

Hypocalcemia

A variety of physical conditions, such as hypoparathyroidism, kidney failure, or lack of Vitamin D can result in insufficient blood levels of calcium.

Calcium is necessary for the function of both the heart and the muscles. An insufficient amount of calcium can result in an irregular heartbeat or muscle spasms, both of which can be interpreted as caused by anxiety or panic.

Hypokalemia

Malnutrition, dehydration, adrenal tumor, hypertension; all can create a lack of potassium in the bloodstream.

Potassium is a major element, required in larger quantities than any other. It is the major ion in fluids found inside the cells. It is critical for normal nerve and muscle function and something as simple as a high salt diet can pull this necessary element out of the cells and interfere with their functioning. A potassium deficiency can result in constipation, nervousness, fatigue, weakness and low blood sugar.

Niacin Deficiency

Niacin is essential in the proper functioning of the blood vessels and in controlling both cholesterol and blood pressure levels.

A niacin deficiency causes mental disturbances almost identical to schizophrenia. Many years ago, psychiatrists distinguished between the two by administering niacin. If the patient recovered, that meant they had pellagra--if not, they were diagnosed as schizophrenic. Niacin deficiencies can produce hallucinations and distortions of perception. A deficiency of this essential vitamin will show up as weakness, fatigue, irritability and insomnia. This vitamin is used up during carbohydrate metabolism and a modern diet of processed food rich in starch (regularly used as thickener) and sugar require that today's diets need an additional niacin intake.

Although an extreme lack of this nutrient is rare today, it is possible for the elderly, drug abusers, alcoholics and those suffering from liver disease to progress to physical manifestations of its shortage.

Vitamin B-12 Deficiency

This vitamin is necessary for the synthesis of DNA and RNA, the stuff of life itself. Cells cannot reproduce without new DNA and RNA being made, and without cell division there is no healing nor growth. RNA is also used by the brain to store information. This RNA function in the brain is thought to be the reason that mental and psychiatric manifestations of B-12 deficiency may long precede any signs of its physical effect--anemia.

Systemic Lupus Erthematosis

SLE or lupus is a chronic disease that involves the inflammation of the body's connective tissue. It is a serious, incurable and unpredictable disease which develops slowly over a period of years. It often begins with a series of fevers that seem to have no apparent point of origin and it ultimately can affect the lungs, spleen, kidneys, and the heart. Common signs include baldness, anemia, the well-known butterfly rash across the bridge of the nose and disfigured joints.

The mental symptoms of lupus are often the first indications that the disease is present. It can mimic all types of mental symptoms, from anxiety to psychosis.

These **metabolic disorders** involve the movement of nutrients after digestion. Because this process is essential to the maintenance of life, any disruption can have severe consequences for the total health of the individual.

Cancers

A diagnosis of any type of cancer can certainly be an anxiety-inducing experience. The thought of the treatments and the possibility of having a terminal disease can contribute to stress in any individual's life.

There are some cancers however, which, because of their location, have the potential to produce primary anxiety symptoms.

Brain Tumor

Symptoms of a tumor of the brain can often include headache, nausea, vomiting, swelling of the optic disk in the eye, weakness and confusion. Sometimes these symptoms, which often cause individuals to believe they are going crazy long before they are diagnosed with a cancerous brain tumor, are sufficient to create extreme anxiety.

Mario's Headache

Mario is a handsome high school senior. Popular and busy, he worked in his parent's neighborhood gas station after school and on the weekends and still had time to belong to the debating society plus play on the basketball team.

When the headaches began, Mario thought he probably was studying too many hours late at night. His parents, immigrants from Cuba, had high aspirations for him and he never wanted to disappoint them.

When nausea and failing vision began to accompany the headaches, he went to the school library to see what he could find to diagnose himself. His search brought him no closer to knowing what the problem was, and he shut the books in disgust. Anxious and sick, he began to avoid his friends and skip basketball practice.

When the headaches became unrelenting, Mario lived in terror because he didn't know what was wrong. He confided in his closest friend that he thought he was going crazy, and then swore his friend to secrecy because he didn't want to embarrass or worry his parents.

By the time Mario was found wandering the school hallways in confusion, he had kept his agony secret from his parents for almost eight months.

Diagnosed with a benign brain tumor, Mario underwent surgery and is a healthy and happy college student today.

Pancreas

Pancreatic cancer often creates problems of mood at the onset. The patient is depressed, given to sudden outbursts of crying and sobbing. This is followed by insomnia which, in itself, contributes to mood changes and depression. The obvious physical symptoms: pain, weight loss, and then jaundice, usually are not visible until the illness has progressed.

Cardiovascular Disorders

Often people who arrive at the emergency room complaining of chest pain will, in fact, be experiencing cardiovascular disease, and not panic disorder. But it is interesting to note that both have very similar symptoms and this very fact often prevents those having a heart attack from seeking medical attention as early as they should.

Mitral Valve Prolapse

The mitral valve separates one of the heart's chambers (the atrium) from the other (the ventricle). Oxygen-rich blood collects in the first one until there is sufficient blood to force the mitral valve open and then the blood flows into the next chamber, the ventricle. From the ventricle the heart pumps oxygen rich blood throughout the entire body.

When the mitral valve doesn't close properly, it allows a small amount of blood to flow back into the atrium. The most common symptoms of this condition are fatigue, difficulty breathing and anxiety.

Mitral valve prolapse is so common that it is estimated that 5 percent of the population have some degree of deficiency in this valve.

The symptoms that accompany this condition are so similar to that of panic disorder that it is listed in *The Diagnostic and Statistical Manual* of the *American Psychiatric Association* as part of the diagnostic criteria for that which should be ruled out before a diagnosis of panic disorder is made.

Myocardial Infarction

MI or myocardial infarction is the fancy term for a heart attack. Usually a blood clot interrupts the flow of blood to the heart and the heart itself is damaged. In some heart attacks the symptoms are severe--a sudden and intense pain that radiates to the neck, arm and upper abdomen.

However, sometimes the symptoms are considerably milder--possible indigestion, a mild discomfort in the area of the collarbone or jaw and an irregular heartbeat. Some of the symptoms, such as the irregular heartbeat, the feeling of being short of breath because the heart is not pumping sufficient oxygenated blood to the brain--which results in a feeling of impending doom--are very similar to those of a panic attack.

It is this type of heart attack that causes some to delay seeking help, afraid of appearing foolish if it is "only" indigestion or stress.

Hypertension

Hypertension or high blood pressure is often without any symptoms. But headaches, ringing in the ears, a feeling of light-headedness and fatigue are some of the vague symptoms that may cause anxiety without producing enough definite symptoms to prompt someone to call the doctor. Instead, many go about their business with this vague feeling that something is wrong. It is possible to continue feeling anxious, worrying without really knowing why, as hypertension continues to progress. It is this lack of definite physical symptoms that causes hypertension to be known as "the silent killer."

Pulmonary Embolism

An artery in the lung can become blocked by tissue, air, fat or a blood clot. Because the lung is blocked, it becomes more and more difficult to breathe. The resulting air hunger and fear can often resemble a heart attack or a panic attack.

Cerebral Arteriosclerosis

The arteries can become thickened, hardened and lose elasticity. As the arteries become narrower it becomes harder to pump blood through them. One of the areas that then finds itself with insufficient oxygen-rich blood is the brain. Arteriosclerosis can be caused by hypertension, diabetes, kidney disease, and elevated cholesterol levels.

Cerebral arteriosclerosis symptoms can resemble those of an anxiety disorder such as headache, dizziness and forgetfulness.

Hemorrhage

A large loss of blood, for whatever reason, will cause rapid pulse, thirst, cold and tingling of hands and feet, dizziness, fainting and a feeling of fear and restlessness.

Of course, any hemorrhage is a medical emergency. However, it does point to the fact that many bodily emergencies have panic-attack-like symptoms.

Endocarditis

An inflammation of the lining or the valves of the heart can be caused by a bacteria. This bacteria can enter the body through a number of routes, sometimes through the mouth by something as simple as a routine cleaning of the teeth at the dentist's office.

In the subacute form of the disease the condition may not be readily diagnosed but the individual may appear to be suffering only from anxiety: with only vague symptoms of weakness, accompanied by loss of appetite, some joint pain and night sweats.

Breathing Disorders

Asthma

The inability to breathe and wheezing, usually caused by a sensitivity to some foreign substance such as dust, pollen, pet dander, etc., or to environmental conditions such as going out into the cold air, stress and extreme exercise, characterizes asthma.

A period of shortness of breath and a tightness in the chest can either be mistaken for an anxiety disorder or create increased anxiety as the individual struggles to breathe.

Bronchitis

An inflammation of the breathing tubes causes them to create mucous. Excess mucous coupled with swollen bronchial tubes makes breathing more and more difficult. Acute bronchitis is usually caused by colds or the flu. Chronic bronchitis (lasting more than six months) is usually caused by a chronic environmental irritant such as cigarette smoke, air pollution or occupational hazards.

Any time someone has difficulty breathing, the brain is receiving less oxygen and the struggle to breathe creates anxiety.

Emphysema

Emphysema is a chronic condition of the tiny air sacs in the lungs. These tiny sacs, known as alveoli, become damaged and no longer allow the individual to breathe out carbon dioxide. Ultimately, this condition leads to lowered oxygen levels and higher carbon dioxide levels.

As the disease progresses, the lungs deteriorate, placing a greater burden on the heart to pump more blood in an effort to remove the carbon dioxide and transport more oxygenated blood to the brain. As a consequence, blood pressure greatly increases and fatigue and depression accompany this effort. Any exertion becomes difficult, increasing the anxiety level of the sufferer.

All the **breathing disorders** have anxiety associated with their manifestation, since it is very normal to become frightened when breathing is difficult. In addition, difficulty in getting one's breath usually includes a reduced oxygen level to the brain.

Psychiatric Conditions

Depression

There are a number of forms of depression which are unique conditions, having nothing to do with anxiety or panic attacks. However, the symptoms often include those of anxiety such as insomnia, fatigue and weight loss.

Bipolar Disorder

This condition, which psychiatry used to call manic depression, is characterized by periods of great activity (the manic phase), alternating with periods of depression. During the manic period there is a decreased need for sleep, increased agitation and increase in goal-directed activity. It is possible to mistake this excessive activity as only anxiety.

A great number of creative individuals in history have been thought to have been manic-depressive, among them: Mozart, Michelangelo, Alexander the Great, Paganini, Lawrence of Arabia, to name a few.

In the manic phase of this disorder, the individual is energetic, filled with euphoria and enthusiasm. The predominant mood is elevated, expansive but sometimes quite irritable. There may be themes of inflated worth, power, knowledge or a special relationship to a deity.

Because this phase is exhilarating and exciting, many resist all efforts toward treatment. They dislike what they call the "lowered emotional state" that most others would call normal. This living on the edge becomes a comfortable state, particularly when the associated symptoms include decreased need for sleep, flight of ideas and goal-directed activity--all thought to be positive attributes for creative artists. In the manic phase the person can become an adrenaline junkie--loving living on the edge.

The depressive phase can bring with it feelings of worthlessness, agitation, decreased energy, difficulty in concentrating and a variety of anxiety symptoms that can appear to be panic.

Seasonal Affective Disorder (SAD)

The winter blues occur for some individuals following a lack of exposure to sunlight, hence the name, given because of the shortened daylight hours during the wintertime. The symptoms are irritability, insomnia, agitation and depression, also all symptoms of anxiety disorders.

Schizophrenia

This mental illness is characterized by a loss of a sense of reality and the inability to think or act normally. While some schizophrenics have delusions and hallucinations, including the hearing of voices, it also includes mood swings, extreme excitement, agitation, fears and social withdrawal.

Personality Disorders

The diagnostic manual of the Psychiatric Association lists sixteen different personality disorders ranging from anti-social to self-defeating personality. These personality disorders are considered to be deeply ingrained ways of interacting with the world that are extremely difficult to change. They can include a rigid way of viewing the world and an inflexible way of thinking that sometimes can impair normal functioning. They are different than the schizophrenics however, in that the individual does not have hallucinations and is usually able to function, although he may find his view of the world extremely limiting. This inflexible view of the world and inability to change can sometimes be a contributing factor in anxiety disorder.

For example, one of the sixteen named personalities is dependent personality. These persons may be so dependent on another that they are unable to leave the house alone--thus they might also be diagnosed as agoraphobic, which is considered as one of the forms of panic attack disorder.

These are just some of the examples of **psychiatric conditions**, many of which overlap, which can mimic anxiety and may be confused with anxiety disorders.

Medication and Drugs

Every drug--prescribed, over-the-counter or illegal--has side effects. No matter how "harmless" it is, it conforms to the law of physics which states: "For every action there is an equal and opposite reaction."

Chemicals of any kind, introduced into the body, affect the body's chemical balance and the brain reacts to these changes. It is entirely possible for chemicals--drugs--to create changes in mood and behavior.

Medications have saved millions of lives and the very power of these medications attests to their success in doing just that. Unfortunately, some people fail to associate their anxiety-like symptoms with their medication.

Every drug, including those properly prescribed for a medical condition, has a list of adverse effects or side effects which the patient may encounter. These adverse effects are listed in a large book known as the PDR or *Physicians Desk Reference* and it is available in any pharmacy. It is a good idea to know just what these side effects are to be prepared for what might occur, no matter how beneficial or necessary the medication might be. A person who regularly takes something prescribed for a condition by the doctor certainly wouldn't want to stop taking this medication, but it is wise to know just what the side effects are.

Antidepressants--Monoamine oxidase inhibitors

These antidepressants work to lift depression because their action is very similar to that of amphetamines and can cause nervousness, insomnia and euphoria. The greater the effect of decreasing the depression, the greater the incidence of anxiety-like side effects.

Bronchial Dilators--Albuterol

This is an example of a beta-adrenergic drug used in an inhaler for the relief of bronchospasm in patients with reversible obstructive airway disease.

The list of its adverse reactions include palpitations, increased blood pressure, tremors, dizziness and nervousness.

Anti-Inflammatories--Indomethacin

This is an example of a nonsteroidal anti-inflammatory agent which is often prescribed for a great variety of inflammatory diseases, such as Rheumatoid arthritis, ankylosing spondylitis, and osteoarthritis. It affords relief of symptoms but does not alter the progressive course of the underlying disease. Its purpose is to relieve pain, reduce fever, swelling and tenderness.

Anxiety is a very common side effect, along with feelings of hostility, disorientation, depression and in some rare cases, psychosis.

These are just a few legitimately-prescribed **medications** that can commonly cause anxiety side effects. Whatever your other medical problems, be aware of just what you can expect in the way of side effects of your prescriptions.

Illegal Drugs

Illegal drugs, just like those prescribed, affect the body's chemistry and trigger changes in the brain.

Marijuana

A well-documented effect of use of this drug is depersonalization, a sense of unreality--a feeling of being detached from self.

This sense of unreality is a common effect felt during panic attacks. Those who have studied panic disorder believe that this depersonalization is a defense mechanism. This sense of detachment may provide some security during attacks by removing the individual from the full experience of the terror. Later, this is thought to be one of the more frightening aspects and often is the one that prompts individuals to move into more severe phobic behavior.

During the marijuana-high, users often consider this detachment non-threatening and pleasant. However, this depersonalization can occur later during a "flash back" and can be a very frightening experience.

Cocaine

Cocaine's effects include increased heart rate, irregular heartbeat, restlessness and increased blood pressure. Cocaine generates a systemic sympathetic response, that part of the nervous system that is involved in the fight-or-flight response.

A survey conducted by a national hot line found that more than 50 percent of callers seeking help for their cocaine addiction reported being terrified by the panic attacks that resulted from their drug use.

When a part of the brain is repeatedly stimulated it lowers the brain's activity threshold, so that there will be a reaction at lowered intake levels. Often these reactions will occur without the euphoria or good-feeling that previously accompanied the initial use of the drug. The user will go directly from use-- to panic.

Amphetamines

Amphetamines are well known as being able to produce increased alertness and a reduced desire for food. Many individuals begin using this class of drugs to stay awake longer--students, long-distance truckers, for example. Their use and abuse by dieters is well documented. The less desirable side effects of their use include palpitations, elevated blood pressure, over stimulation, hyperactivity--all anxiety symptoms.

Narcotics withdrawal

Any withdrawal from a drug that creates dependency will cause severe anxiety-like symptoms.

When experiencing a withdrawal crisis addicts will often conceal drug use, adding to the difficulty in treating the anxiety/panic symptoms.

Legal Drugs

Although most of us know that alcohol, nicotine and caffeine are drugs, many people think that because they are legal they are relatively harmless.

Thousands of families whose lives have been destroyed by alcohol abuse know that this is untrue.

Alcohol

Researchers have estimated that of all patients hospitalized for treatment of alcoholism, between 18 to 32 percent may be suffering with panic disorder, agoraphobia or social phobia.

It is well documented that many people drink to calm down, "steady their nerves," ease uncomfortable social situations, relax after a stressful day and, in small doses, alcohol has just that desired effect.

Alcohol is the quickest way to stop a panic attack. For that reason, many panic patients have alcohol available to them at all times. They take a drink as soon as they feel an attack beginning. This attempt at self-medication often leads to addiction.

Research indicates that many alcoholics develop abnormal fears before their drinking problems, suggesting that they have begun drinking to escape from fears and then find themselves trapped in an increased-fear--drink-to-relieve-it--increased-fear cycle.

As this cycle repeats itself, more and more alcohol is required to overcome the fear or panic effects in their lives. Then, the use of alcohol to relieve panic attacks appears to make subsequent attacks all the more possible.

Research indicates that "severely" phobic patients develop alcohol dependency much more quickly than the less phobic. Alcohol soon becomes a factor in anxiety disorders, strengthening the symptoms and prolonging their disastrous effects. In one study the subjects reported that their phobias had begun before their drinking problems and that their fears and anxieties were worse after they were recognized as alcoholic.

To compound the difficulty created by the use of alcohol to mask the symptoms of panic, the symptom of alcohol withdrawal is--an increase in panic symptoms!

Withdrawal from alcohol causes the brain to go through increased excitability. Depending upon the length of time that the individual has been using alcohol, this can include hyper-nervousness and go as far as delirium tremens--which can include terrifying hallucinations.

Nicotine

Anyone who has tried to stop smoking knows just how difficult this is. Researchers have likened nicotine addiction to heroin addiction. Withdrawal symptoms include irritability, tension, anxiety, cravings, shaking--all panic disorder symptoms. Even those who have attempted to reduce their nicotine levels by reducing their use find they have panic symptoms at lower levels.

Caffeine

All of caffeine's symptoms closely reflect the body's physical response to fear: increased pulse, heart rate, blood pressure, sensory acuity, muscle contraction and alertness.

In addition to the nerve jangling effects of the caffeine in coffee, tea and cola drinks, researchers at the University of California at Irvine have discovered that individuals who suffer from panic attacks are three times more sensitive to the bitter taste of coffee than others. Edward DeMet, the head of the study, speculates that panic-attack patients suffer from a dysfunction of adenosine. Adenosine is a chemical that regulates taste and stimulates the nerve cells in the heart and brain to react.

This adenosine dysfunction to bitter taste is in addition to the caffeine stimulation of the nervous system which coffee provides. Dr. DeMet suggests that all individuals who are sensitive to coffee avoid it in all its forms, including de-caffeinated.

Researchers at Yale and the National Institute of Mental Health found that fifteen of twenty-one patients suffering from agoraphobia reported symptoms similar to those of panic attacks after receiving a caffeine dose equal to eight cups of coffee. Four cups of coffee brought on symptoms in 40 percent of those patients.

These researchers believe caffeine may inhibit the action of adenosine, which reduces spontaneous firing of neurons in the brain. The drug yohimbine, which is often taken by men who suffer from problems of impotence, has similar effects. Both substances may increase the amount of calcium in neurons, which could inhibit the action of adenosine. This reduction in adenosine increased brain activity in response to stimulation, with a subsequent release of adrenaline.

Further confirmation of these studies was made by University of Arizona psychiatrist Michael F. Breslow who confirmed that as little as one can of cola or one cup of coffee can trigger an anxiety attack in susceptible individuals.

Coffee Madness--Bitter Jitters

Kathleen was a non-stop talker. She started talking to her cat Fluffball first thing in the morning. Often she drank several cups of coffee in the morning. When she got to work she filled her cup before she headed to her desk. She kept up her rapid-fire witticisms on her job, all day long. She was known for her clever tongue and her ability to put down with a well-turned phrase anybody who chose to verbally duel with her.

"People were always suggesting that I should be working at a comedy club somewhere. I loved that. It made me feel bright and clever."

By the middle of the afternoon, Kathleen's alertness would begin to wear off. "I would drink 4 or 5 cups to get myself 'up' again. That certainly would improve my performance--I could blast through the afternoon and be ready to go out and dance that evening."

Sometimes Kathleen would feel edgy, nervous and restless. Sometimes, while she was attempting to be clever, she found that she was sweating, breathing rapidly with a pounding heart and had a pounding headache. "I would end the conversation and run outside, laughing like a maniac so that people would just think I was being silly.

"Actually, I had to get outside so I could breathe and get myself under control again. I knew that I was having panic attacks. But I never ever saw any connection to them and my coffee drinking. Who would have thought they were caused by caffeine. I just thought coffee make me more energetic, gave me more of a glib tongue."

"Society has found some of these symptoms desirable because we all think that coffee (and caffeine) gives us an 'edge,' improves performance. We live in a very competitive society which to me means 'live in fear': meet the deadline, make that first impression, make the grade, the cut, the team-- it's all craziness.

"I'm not so witty anymore because now I only drink herbal tea. I feel a lot better and the trade off for my mental health is well worth it," says Kathleen.

Aspartame

Recent research has implicated this artificial sweetener as having a possible link to seizures, migraine headaches and other psychiatric symptoms.

TO THINK IS TO PRACTICE BODY CHEMISTRY-- THERE IS A MOLECULAR RESPONSE TO EVERY THOUGHT.

While this may sound impossible at this point, read on--and you will begin to understand the meaning of this statement.

Over-The-Counter Medications

Modern drug stores, variety stores, shopping warehouses, even the grocery store--they all have shelf after shelf of "harmless" products. After all, if they were dangerous you would need a prescription for them, wouldn't you?

In the section on prescription drugs we made mention of the *Physicians' Desk Reference* or PDR, the handbook available in all public libraries and pharmacies that gives details on the latest information concerning the side effects, adverse reactions and contraindications for thousands of drugs.

What many people don't know is that there is an identical publication, known as the *Physicians' Desk Reference for Non-prescription Drugs*, which is also available in the local library or pharmacy. It contains the same information on over-the-counter drugs--those things we often buy without much thought--for a headache, a backache, a stuffy nose or an upset stomach.

Advertisers spend countless millions of dollars promoting these products. Glossy magazines have

pages of beautiful photos and words written by professionals in advertising agencies; television has
fantastic productions with a visual message that these
products are the simple answer to daily problems--
just take a pill and you'll eliminate the problem--and
none of these venues tell us about side effects.

Diet pills

Billions of dollars are spent annually on diet
products in an effort to painlessly lose weight. While
diet pills do not contain amphetamines, their ingredients often do include stimulants, sometimes an
excessive dose of caffeine, and often phenyl-
propanolamine (a so-called non-prescription appetite suppressant); these stimulants can mimic the
effects of amphetamines. Hundreds of persons with
adverse reactions to these products find their way to
emergency rooms annually.

Mary's Fear of Bugs

When Mary was a young girl, she was
stung on the foot by a wasp. She had quite
a reaction. Her foot was swollen for several
days and the pain was intense. When it happened, she had run home screaming and it
was minutes before her mother could calm
her enough to even find out what was wrong.
When her shoe and sock came off, the dead

wasp was found trapped there and that set Mary off again, screaming and hiding her face in her mother's lap.

Mary equates her fear of all bugs to that incident, which she remembers very clearly. "During the spring there are so many caterpillars hanging from the trees and the eaves of the house that you can hardly leave home without one falling on you. I can't stand it. My legs start to shake and I have to run back into the house. I'm almost crazy before I can get the caterpillar off me." Mary had begun to work on her bug phobia and thought she was doing quite well.

Mary knew that she felt more nervous when she took diet pills, but she took them anyway since she felt she simply couldn't control her weight without help.

When Mary found ants in her kitchen, she absolutely went berserk. "I was running frantically, running into things. Anything, to get away from those bugs."

When Mary slammed into the doorway, breaking her arm in her panic, she ended up in the emergency room. "I was ready to pass out--it was beyond anything I had ever experienced before. When the doctor in the emergency room examined me, he couldn't believe my heart rate. I told him about what had happened and I just casually mentioned that I was regularly taking an over-the-counter diet pill. This doctor was very straight forward with me. He told me just what the diet pills were doing to both my heart rate and my nerves. I finally had to realize that someone like me, with a phobia, just has to avoid chemicals that add to my nervousness, increase my anxiety reaction--but it took breaking my arm for me to learn that lesson."

Mary stopped taking diet pills, joined Weight Watchers and learned how to eat properly. "Not only did stopping the diet pills help me, eating properly and getting the right nutrients made a world of difference. I have lost most of the weight I wanted to lose, I think I am going to be able to keep it off and--I can almost control my phobia about bugs! I'm working on that now."

Pain killers

Headache remedies and pain killers, sinus medications for the relief of nasal congestion, runny nose, itching eyes; products for the relief of upper respiratory allergies; these are other over-the-counter medicines bought annually by the billions of dollars' worth.

Some of them contain pseudoephedrine, a product which may cause excitability. Sometimes the warnings on these remedies include statements such as: higher doses can cause nervousness, dizziness or sleeplessness. Bad news if you already suffer from panic disorder.

Ed's Constant Headache

"I know that I appear to be calm and in control of myself, but inside I'm quaking. I do OK on a one-to-one basis with people, even strangers, but in a group of people I not only feel trapped, I start getting a headache and begin to panic. Whenever I find myself in some kind of a group situation I am almost tongue-tied. I try to participate in the group and say something, I really do-- but whatever I say seems to come out sounding so stupid I could just die. I look around at the people and they are looking at me with blank faces. Oh, then, I just wish the earth would open up and swallow me.

"I do the best I can on my job but I am intensely anxious most of the time. Each day is a struggle and I am constantly worried that I will be asked to speak out about something. As I get older, the struggle gets harder and harder.

"When the headaches got worse, I began taking a headache medicine every night--and then I couldn't sleep. The next day things were so much worse for me. I felt anxious, dizzy and panicky. Of course, that just increased my anxiety and my headache. I just don't know where it will end.

"My doctor says I shouldn't take these medicines for headaches, that they have side effects that are bad for me. But then I just have to suffer with the headache and the panic, which my doctor says is a social phobia. I've had a brain scan and a bunch of other tests, to see if there was anything physical causing my headaches but apparently there isn't. What happens is that when I get tense I tighten up the muscles in my neck and shoulders and this constriction of the blood vessels creates my headaches."

Ed has had a physical examination and diagnosis. Ed is a definite candidate for professional help. He needs help to deal with his personality problems, lack of self-esteem, headaches and social phobia. It is time for Ed to take action before things become worse for him--he definitely has the potential to move from social phobia to agoraphobia.

Night time cold preparations

A night time cold preparation lists the following warning: Do not take this produce if you have asthma, emphysema, chronic pulmonary disease, shortness of breath, difficulty in breathing. A person with panic disorder already feels as if they are suffocating. Having a panic disorder shortly after ingesting one of these products can be terrifying.

Thousands of different products and brands, all easily available for the relief of something or other-- but beware: that relief could bring the symptoms of anxiety. There could be adverse effects lurking there for susceptible individuals.

The Environment

For the delicately balanced brain chemistry, the presence of even small amounts of toxic elements may trigger a variety of mental disturbances.

Mercury

Industrial settings are often a source of mercury vapor. Skin products, laxatives and even douches can contain mercury-based ingredients. The psychiatric symptoms of mercury toxicity include xenophobia (an abnormal fear of strangers) and anxiety, as well as depression, mood swings and irritability.

Carbon Dioxide

The inhalation of carbon dioxide has been shown to provoke panic-like anxiety in patients who are already prone to panic disorders. It appears that panic sufferers are more sensitive to carbon dioxide than the rest of the population. Studies point out that carbon dioxide over-stimulates certain centers in the brain, especially in the locus ceruleus, which is thought to be important in panic attacks.

Volatile Substances

Painters, workers in refineries, members of airport refueling teams and other individuals who work in industries where they are routinely exposed to volatile substances can have bouts of anxiety, along with personality changes, depression and other psychiatric symptoms.

Insecticides

In humans, inhalation of, or prolonged contact with, pest-destroying chemicals which contain organophosphates, can block the production of an essential brain enzyme. The physical results include anxiety, irritability, depression, restlessness and decreased memory and attention span.

PART II

What Causes this Problem?

Chapter 4
Who Gets Panic Disorders?

Genetics

Panic disorder appears to run in families. One study has shown that if one twin in a genetically identical pair has panic disorder, it is likely that the other twin will also suffer from the disorder. Fraternal, or non-identical, twin pairs do not show this high degree of "concordance" with respect to panic disorder. Thus it appears that genetic factors, in combination with environmental factors, may be responsible for vulnerability to this condition.

At the National Institute for Mental Health scientists have been studying families in which several individuals have panic disorder. The aim of these studies is to identify the specific gene or genes involved in the condition. Should such genes be identified this could lead to even more new approaches for diagnosing and treating panic disorder.

Jumping Frenchmen of Maine

It is an unusual name for a disorder, it gets your attention right away. The National Organization of

Rare Disorders lists "Jumping Frenchmen of Maine" in their database as a disorder characterized by an unusually extreme startle reaction. This disorder was first identified during the late nineteenth century in Maine and the Canadian province of Quebec. Lumberjacks of French Canadian descent were originally associated with this phenomenon but it has been observed in other societies in many parts of the world as well. In Malaysia it is known as Latah and in Siberia as Myriachit.

It is considered a genetic disorder of hereditary neurological origin and/or an extreme conditioned response to a particular situation influenced by cultural factors. This extreme startle response is even more intense if the individual is tired or anxious.

There are related extreme startle response disorders. Tourette Syndrome, another hereditary neurological disorder, is characterized by involuntary muscular movements and uncontrollable vocal sounds.

Less well known are Hyperplexia, Startle Epilepsy and Kok Disease, wherein individuals have an excessive startle reaction to sudden unexpected noise, as well as unexpected movement or touch.

Do people with panic disorder have any of these disorders? Probably not. But, if we can accept that these neurological conditions can be hereditary and are the result of a discrete biochemical abnormality in the brain, which consequently creates a cascade of anxiety-related bodily reactions, such as muscle tension, increased heart rate and anxiety, it is easier to understand that there can be all kinds of variations in the make-up of the very complex human body--which then can result in an excessive reaction to anxiety provoking thoughts and situations.

The Biological Component

The human body has an extremely elaborate and efficient communication network. This network includes the central nervous system (the brain and the spinal cord) and the peripheral nervous system (the remaining network of nerves). The central nervous system operates by billions of electrical impulses traveling along its pathways, carrying sensory input from our senses (hearing, sight, touch, smell) to the brain and relaying instructions from the brain back to the body, telling it how to respond to that information.

The basic working unit of the central nervous system is the neuron, a specialized cell with the ability to generate and transmit electrical impulses. Chains of neurons form the pathways along which impulses travel on their way to the appropriate regions of the brain. Impulses from the ear travel along the auditory nerve to the superior temporal lobe of the brain where they are translated into sound. Impulses from the eye travel along the optic nerve to the occipital lobe of the brain where they are translated into visual images. Exactly how this translation takes place is a mystery, but brain chemicals called neurotransmitters are involved in the translation.

Neurotransmitters regulate the transmission of impulses between neurons. One kind of neurotransmitter acts as a "stop" signal, blocking the transmission of an impulse, and others act as a "go" signal, telling the impulses that they can cross to the next neuron.

These chemical neurotransmitters have a role in every iota of sensory input to the brain. They have a role in every brain activity, including sleep, pleasure, pain, all thought transmission, emotions and the responses to emotions.

Certain areas of the brain have been pinpointed as having to do with a variety of emotional responses. For example, the locus ceruleus is known to be associated with fear responses and this brain area contains an abundance of noradrenergic neurotransmitters.

Norepinephrine, also known as noradrenaline, is produced by the adrenal gland after it gets a message from the brain to do so. This is the chemical that stimulates the heart muscle, accelerates the heart rate and increases cardiac output. An increase in messages to the adrenals to increase their adrenergic production will also have as a result the raising of anxiety levels, along with the increased heart rate. Experiments in which drugs were given to stimulate the transmitters to increase their flow increased anxiety. Drugs that inhibit the flow decreased anxiety.

Various researchers believe the flaw lies in the chemistry of the brain itself. Their studies indicate that overly sensitive chemoreceptors may be at fault. Panic disorder may be associated with increased activity in the hippocampus and locus ceruleus, as these portions of the brain monitor all external and internal stimuli and control the brain's responses to them. If neurotransmitters send a message that there is danger, the brain will respond with the appropriate chemicals, sending them throughout the body so that each nerve fiber will do its part in preparing the body to either run or defend itself. It has been well documented that panic disorder patients have increased activity in the adrenergic system, which we have already learned regulates such physiological functions as heart rate and temperature.

Individuals who are prone to panic attacks often have elevated levels of lactic acid in their bloodstreams.

Researchers at the Washington University School of Medicine believe that this is the physiological basis for panic disorder. Positron emission tomography of patients with the disorder illustrate that there is an unequal flow of blood to the parahippocampal gyrus, a region of the brain that is thought to mediate anxiety. These researchers believe that the blood-brain barrier may be slightly defective in these patients, allowing substances such as lactate to reach the brain, thus inducing an attack.

Another group of studies at the NIMH suggests that people with panic disorder may have abnormalities in their benzodiazepine receptors, brain components that react with anxiety-reducing substances within the brain.

In conducting this research, scientists can use several different techniques to provoke panic attacks in individuals who have documented panic disorder, uncomplicated with a medical condition that exhibits some of the similar symptoms. The best known method to provoke panic attacks is an intravenous administration of sodium lactate, the same chemical that normally builds up in the muscles during heavy exercise.

Dr. Donald Klein, professor of psychiatry at Columbia University, believes panic attacks may be a result of a defect in the way the brain warns against suffocation. The human brain's warning system fires whenever the amount of carbon dioxide in the blood becomes too high, a sign of oxygen deprivation. In some people, an overly sensitive system fires a false alarm that then sets off a cascade of events which culminate in a panic attack. Hyperventilation and breathing air with a higher-than-usual level of carbon dioxide can also trigger attacks in people with panic disorder.

Other substances that have been shown to trigger panic attacks in susceptible people include caffeine (generally 5 or more cups of coffee are required).

Because such provocations generally do NOT trigger panic attacks in people who do not have the disorder, scientists have inferred that individuals who have panic disorder are some how biologically different from people who do not.

It probably isn't important which of these biological factors are at the physiological root of panic disorder. It is sufficient to know that in some individuals such an overly reactive brain chemistry is sending out a false alarm. The message the body is sending probably isn't accurate and just this knowledge, that there may be some biological basis for the disorder, should be comforting to many.

In addition, it is also true that when people prone to panic attacks are told in advance about the sensations these provocations with sodium lactate and carbon dioxide will cause, they are much less likely to panic. This suggests that there is also a strong psychological component, as well as the biological one, in panic disorder.

Many people experience triggering events such as periods of high stress at work. Some develop panic disorder and agoraphobia, others do not. What separates those who do develop the anxiety/panic cycle from those who do not seems to be the personality traits. People with high anxiety personality traits are more likely to exaggerate the meaning of the initial symptoms, begin to watch their bodies carefully, worry about what the symptoms mean and what might happen if they cannot be controlled. In essence, anxiety becomes a kind of "black cloud" hanging over their heads. They run from any sign of the black cloud on the horizon. Unfortunately, most of the symptoms they are running away from are quite normal. The key to the development of the anxiety/panic cycle is what the individual believes about the external factors that are impacting them.

Results of Animal Studies

NIMH-sponsored researchers are studying anxiety in animals in an effort to find clues to the underlying causes of anxiety. One series of studies involved an inbred line of pointer dogs that exhibited extreme, abnormal fearfulness when approached by humans or that startled excessively by loud noises. In contrast with normal pointers, these nervous dogs have been found to react more strongly to caffeine and to have brain tissue that is richer in receptors for adenosine, a naturally occurring sedative that normally exerts a calming effect within the brain. Further study of these animals is expected to reveal how a genetic predisposition toward anxiety is expressed in their brains.

Other animal studies involve macaque monkeys. Some of these animals exhibit anxiety when given an infusion of lactate, much like people with panic disorder. Other macaques do not exhibit this response. Scientists conducting these studies are attempting to determine how the brains of the responsive and nonresponsive monkeys differ. Hopefully, this research should provide additional information concerning the causes of panic disorder.

In addition, research with rats is exploring the effects of various medications on the parts of the brain involved in anxiety.

Further, scientists funded by NIMH are investigating the basic thought processes and emotions that come into play during a panic attack and those that contribute to the development and persistence of agoraphobia. These studies on the cognitive factors in panic disorders will evaluate the impact of various therapies to determine if some variants are more

or which individuals. The research pro-
so explore the effects of interpersonal
as marital conflict on the disorder.

The Role of Diet

It seems silly to think that diet could be a contributory factor in creating panic attacks but if we think
that all bodily chemistry is the result of chemical
interactions within the cells, then it seems apparent
that these chemicals must come from somewhere.
Just as gasoline fuels an automobile, food fuels the
body.

Dr. Michael Lesser, a psychiatrist who special-
izes in nutritional medicine says, "Ninety-two percent of the patients who come to see me with symptoms
such as anxiety, fatigue, palpitations, fears, trem-
bling--all the symptoms of panic disorder and pho-
bia--had abnormal blood sugar test results. I firmly
believe that abnormalities in blood sugar have a direct physiological correlation to the symptoms."

Dr. Lesser always administers a five-or-six-hour
glucose tolerance test to all patients exhibiting such
symptoms and suggests that all physicians who see
patients with these symptoms do the same. If you
have not had such a test, you should have one before
you look any further for the reasons for your mental
distress.

The Psychological Component

Psychologists have argued for years over "nature vs nurture." One group of theorists says that the personality is almost completely the result of nature-- that is, genetically endowed. Your heritage predicts what type of person you will be: you can thank your parents (or curse them) for the way you are.

Another group of theorists maintains that nurture is mainly responsible for the kind of person you are. That is, your school and your peers all impact on this blank slate and the result of those experiences creates your personality.

The majority of theorists however, suggest that inherited traits are impacted upon by the environment. There are differing theories about how much of each are important. Some say that genetics accounts for as much as sixty percent; others claim that the percentage of impact is higher for the environment. Whatever the percentages, they feel that personality is the result of both of these things coming together, inherited traits and the environment, which ultimately results in the final "personality" of the individual.

It is known that individuals who have difficulties related to anxiety share many of the same personality traits. Some of these traits are highly desirable but can be taken to extremes.

General Personality Traits

These traits may or may not apply to you. Or you may think that they describe individuals whom you know do not suffer from anxiety. These are only traits and sometimes in combination they are balancing, or in effect cancel each other out. But--the presence of some of these contribute to the type of personality groupings that are often a part of the personality of highly anxious individuals:

Creative-imaginative

The ability to visualize vividly. This is the wonderful creativeness that makes it possible to imagine a play, create a drama, tell a fairy tale to a child so realistically that the child imagines him or herself to be in this fantasy land of words. The ability to visualize vividly can be destructive too, creating in the mind the awful possibilities that could occur in the future. The "what if" landscape of fear can result from this imagination.

Rigid

Events are only black and white, right or wrong, fair or unfair. This trait in the personality causes the individual to create a lot "rules" of behavior which apply not only to others but to themselves.

Low self-esteem

The newspapers are full of stories of youngsters

who end up in trouble with the law because they don't think they are good enough to go to school or that they deserve a chance. This lack of self-worth is considered a learned characteristic. A child is told repeatedly that she hasn't done well enough or that he isn't good enough. Low self-esteem individuals depend on others for their sense of self-worth, they don't really "know" with any security that they are good or worthwhile. The hunger for approval is so excessive and the fear of rejection is so strong that this individual is overly sensitive to criticism and has great difficulty in saying "no" to the demands of others. They make great friends because they often make it their responsibility to keep others happy.

Perfectionist

The perfectionists expect greater performance and accomplishment from themselves than they would ever expect from others. Everything has to be perfect. This thinking creates all-or-nothing attitudes about their own actions. The perfectionist can beat themselves over the head over small errors or lapses in judgement that others would hardly notice. This causes the perfectionist to consider anything that is less than absolutely perfect a failure. And how often can anything be absolutely perfect? So the stage is set for self-disappointment.

Controller

Everything must be predictable. Unexpected change is the beginning of stress. Because it is harder to know just what others will do, the controller needs to control everyone and everything.

Capable/dependable

Everyone likes the person who can "get the job done." We all admire these persons and want to be just like them. But, when this edges into perfectionism, rigid thinking about how things should be done, and a need to control all situations, the stage is set for high anxiety when a capable and dependable person can't get the job done because of outside factors.

Suppressor of bodily signals

The trait is prevalent in the person who will keep on going, even when he or she doesn't feel well, is hurting or exhausted. The body becomes secondary to the task and its demands for rest or treatment are often ignored or given a very low priority. Someone with this trait will show up for work feeling a lot worse than someone else who has called in sick and is rewarded with praise for having done so. The result--symptoms of fatigue are only admitted when exhaustion is about to overcome the individual.

It is quite possible as you read the traits you said to yourself, "That's me." If that is so, it is also very possible that these traits work to your disadvantage when it comes to having the kind of high-anxiety personality that predisposes to panic disorder.

It is obvious that these personality traits are not necessarily negative. Problem solving is done by creative individuals. Everyone needs approval and it is the basis for fulfilling relationships. High personal expectations lead to greater performance. Dependability is at the core of the work ethic. Each of these traits will have a high and low end. Individuals with anxiety-related difficulties tend to be at the extreme. Difficulties arise when these traits become exaggerated and pass out of the healthy range into the obsessive.

An awareness of these traits is the beginning of understanding how they impact on panic disorders and learning to use them appropriately is part of the solution to learning to end panic attacks.

Chapter 5
How Does Personality Develop?

Stages

The newborn baby is completely helpless, but he is also utterly selfish. The only thing that matters to him is that his needs are satisfied. For years he cannot really distinguish between himself and his environment. He thinks he is the world; at the same time he realizes that he is powerless. This paradox of egocentricity and complete dependency is but the first in a series of conflicts the child must resolve. In doing so he establishes the feelings about the world and the image of himself that we call personality. Later, when he reaches adolescence, he will have to revise his self-image and integrate new feelings into his childhood personality.

Attachment

Nature supplies the infant with a mother who is able to care for her. The newborn's few activities-- sucking, clinging, crying--serve to attach the baby to her mother, and the mother to her baby. The infant clings to her mother when she holds her; this triggers in the mother the desire to protect and provide for the child. Her mother satisfies her need for food; she begins to view her mother in a positive way and thus forms the first social attachment of her life. Parents also give her warmth and "contact comfort," and they talk to her and smile at her. Clearly, these are all important to the child's development.

Autonomy

As soon as they are able to crawl, infants begin to leave their mothers--if only briefly. Exploration and separation are essential to the development of any child. If he remained at his mother's side all the time, he would never learn to do things for himself; he would never develop a sense of autonomy.

Some psychologists feel that toilet training determines the child's feelings about authority, discipline, and self-control. Toilet training usually begins before the child can talk and understand reasons. If he is pushed too fast, he begins to feel he is a weak and disappointing person. In later childhood he may react to authority and demands with "anxious conformity," trying desperately to please or with "negativism," rejecting all demands so as to avoid failure.

A child at this stage faces a number of constraints--eating at a particular time, learning that he may be able to get away with hitting another child in the stomach but not with stepping on his head, that he can play with father's pencils but not with his coin collection, and so on. In working out each conflict between his desires and parental rules, the child establishes feelings about himself and the world.

During adolescence the drive for independence and autonomy becomes stronger. This is a necessary part of growing up in our society, where people are often geographically separated from their parents and must be able to solve their own problems. Most adolescents do desire the external symbols of independence and most parents seem fairly willing to respond to these wishes.

The transition to emotional independence and self-direction is far from easy.

Imitation and Identification

One of the ways a child solves conflicts is by imitating and identifying with the adults in her life. Parents, other adults, older siblings--and television-- all provide her with models of acceptable behavior.

Identification may take a number of forms. The child may adopt her parents' characteristics because this may bring her love. Or she may fear rejection and punishment if she does not follow their model. Identification may also help the child overcome fear and frustration. If she identifies with her parents' commands, the commands begin to seem less fear-invoking.

The child also looks to adults--especially her parents--for clues as to what she can reasonably expect from life. Children are constantly being told that there are some things adults may do that children may not do, and this is frustrating. The child works around these prohibitions in play and fantasy, by unconsciously identifying with "big people" and living through them. In this way she can take on some of the adults' apparent omnipotence.

This is particularly important in the learning of sex roles. In the beginning, both boys and girls identify most with their mothers, but while the girl may go on modeling herself after her mother, at some point the boy is expected to switch over to his father. Sometimes this transition is successful--the boy who sees his father as nurturing may be more willing to "give up" his mother. Other times--for example, when the father is the parent who administers discipline and punishment--the child identifies with his father in a defensive way and will cling to his mother longer than is considered appropriate. At a later stage, the girl begins to look at her father for confirmation of her feminine role.

Peer Groups

In our society, children generally have few meaningful social relationships outside their family for their first 4 or 5 years. They may play with other children, but usually their mother is close at hand. School changes all this. The child's world is suddenly filled with "significant others"--his peers and teachers. The number of models for him to imitate and identify with increases. He finds he has lost some of the attention and freedom he had at home; he has to cope with other children's desires and aggression.

Gradually he transfers some of the feelings of attachment he worked out at home to his teachers and peer group. He begins to look to them as well as to his parents for approval. He asks his teacher to help him reach a goal; later he asks his friends. He begins to join groups. By adolescence the peer group has assumed primary importance. It seems that the adolescent compensates for his increasing independence from his parents by clinging to his friends until he feels more confident about being on his own. Unfortunately, however, his peers do not always give him the support he needs. The high school has been aptly called "a cruel jungle of dating and rating," a place where only the fittest survive socially. Those who don't measure up find themselves left out, and the pressure to be "in" and the fear of being "out" can cause far greater emotional strain than the academic pressure parents typically worry about.

Even the socially successful adolescent may not be completely comfortable with his peers. Adolescents have their own subculture, with its own set of values, and these values are often very different from those of the family. Attitudes toward sex, drugs, alcohol, and grades are among the many possible sources of conflict. Adolescents must reconcile the two worlds of family and peers. They must sort out the numerous and often conflicting expectations of others and decide which values are really their own.

Development of Identity

A child has many fragmented "selves"--daughter, sister, friend, "Fatso," baseball player, whiner, artist, and so forth. As an adolescent, that same individual becomes capable of integrating these many roles into a single, unified identity. To form a coherent self-concept, she must evaluate and choose from the vast number of beliefs, values, and rules available in modern society. This self-concept must have continuity with the past and the future--with what she already knows about herself and what she can reasonably expect to become.

In simpler times, career, life style, and personal philosophies were largely determined by family background. There were clearly defined standards for sex roles and morality. In short, the adolescent had relatively few life choices to make. But our society has become increasingly complex and mobile and now offers a bewildering number of occupations, life styles, ideologies, and sex-role models. Today's adolescent can be nearly anything she wants to be, but choosing from so many alternatives can be extremely difficult. She must experiment with numerous roles and behaviors and must test herself in as many situations as possible. But eventually she must choose and integrate her choices into a whole, healthy personality. She must figure out who she is and how she fits in with or up against the world around her.

This "quest for the identity" is the principal task of adolescence.

Transition to Adulthood

The phenomena that introduce adolescence are biological and thus they are universal. But the phenomena that mark the end of adolescence and the beginning of adulthood are psychosocial and are thus determined by the individual and his culture. Adult status is not bestowed by an act of nature. In our culture it is not very clear how or when this is earned; there is no clear-cut border to cross. The principal test of adulthood appears to be creating something meaningful and permanent to perpetuate self, and for this reason children and work become major concerns for most adults. With productivity comes a sense of fulfillment. Personality in the middle years is characterized by the establishment of a balance between the internal self and social roles. The adult develops a sense not only of who he is but also of how he relates to his society.

Development of States of High Anxiety

As we just discussed, personality is formed by the interaction of: the methods used to train and socialize the individual; the role models observed ; the values and beliefs of the core family; the individual's place within the family; the social and cultural influences; and biology.

Dr. Katherine Shear, professor of psychiatry at the University of Pittsburgh, feels that biological predisposition exists in panic attacks but that these attacks don't happen without certain kinds of early experience and psychic conflict. In other words, biology and early experience conspire to produce panic. She states that panic disorders are the result of neurophysiological irritability at birth, the feeling of being threatened and/or suffocated by parental behavior during childhood, and upsetting trauma in early adulthood.

These factors can interact in a variety of ways during the formation of the personality. Some researchers theorize that panic attacks are essentially rooted in childhood psychological trauma. For some, one factor can have more significance than another, but individuals who exhibit the high anxiety profile seem to have been adversely impacted upon by some of the following:

Alcoholism

There are many similarities between the traits of those with panic disorder and those who are adult children of alcoholics. It is certainly understandable that being raised in a home where alcoholism controls one or more of the adults might result in a child who is unsure, fearful and unable to trust others.

Abuse

Physical abuse, including unusual punishments.
Sexual abuse.
Psychological abuse such as name calling, belittling or threats of abandonment.
Emotional neglect.

Many adults who have experienced abuse have often spent their formative years not developing, only surviving. Only surviving may require coping skills that call on only those that are self-protecting, rather than those that round out the personality. In a household where there is screaming and yelling, physical violence and threats of abandonment, a child needs to develop some problem solving strategies to deal with all that. The child may develop very rigid rules of behavior to create a sense of security in the midst of this chaos. It is highly possible that these individuals will have a high potential for anxiety disorders.

Role models

The role models presented by the parents or significant others in the childhood of someone with a high anxiety profile certainly may well include modeling of anxiety as the way to be.

Perfectionist parents may have unrealistic expectations and demand adult behavior or the performance of tasks beyond the skills of the child. This might include an expectation that the child will always behave properly and not embarrass the family. Sometimes approval is only given when something is accomplished. Good grades, performing household duties, learning to play a musical instrument, are examples of the kinds of things that garner approval. If only performance-related approval is given it encourages the belief that the person is of little value, only the performance is. Attempting to live up to high standards set by this kind of perfectionism can create an environment where the child can only fail and then feel inadequate and worthless. In addition, the child learns that she must continuously perform to be loved.

Role modeling by siblings often can include teasing and criticism that borders on abuse.

Rigid conformity requirements may set the stage for a pattern of thinking that everything is either black or white and there are no in-betweens to be considered. This rigid belief system may come from a particular cultural background or a religious affiliation and can become a most important model for rigid thinking.

Required dependency by parents who protect the child from the adversities of life is sometimes only fulfilling the need of the parents to have someone dependent on them. This kind of overprotection encourages the thinking that any kind of risk taking is dangerous and should be avoided. The consequence of this is that the child is prevented from learning to handle adversity and that there are risks in any kind of judgement making.

"Don't cry," or "That is a terrible way to feel," or "How can you be so mean," are statements from parents that send the message that the child should suppress feelings. When a child is told the feelings expressed are not important or that, "You don't really feel that way," the child learns to deny emotions.

Sometimes it is not possible for the parent to always be there for the child. Legitimate reasons such as hospitalization, divorce or death are not often understood by the child and can create feelings of worthlessness, anxiety and abandonment.

There are also occasions when the child must assume an adult role. It could be that the parent has a lengthy absence or a serious illness requiring hospitalization, and a child must care for younger siblings, manage the household, or even care for the ill adult. This role reversal puts the child into a situation of assuming adult responsibilities long before the child is mature enough to do so. A child who assumes such responsibilities often develops a rigid set of rules in order to meet these adult demands. Prolonged absences of a parent can create a separation anxiety, particularly when the child does not understand the reason for the absence. If the absence is not explained it can cause the child to feel unloved and abandoned.

There are occasions when the family energy is centered on a family secret. This is typical in the households of alcoholics where the entire family covers the alcoholic behavior by lying to the employer, making excuses for social lapses--such as violent behavior--and "pretending" that nothing is wrong. Such enabling behavior generates the belief within the family structure that certain feelings are wrong and must be suppressed or hidden. Such a family creates an environment that says it is OK to lie to protect behavior in both others and self.

Traits

If someone is asked to describe a certain person, most often they would probably identify certain behavior patterns or traits. Thus, to the question, "What kind of a person is John?" the reply would be that he is moody or friendly, aggressive or reserved, energetic or lazy--whatever characteristic types of behavior he has most frequently exhibited.

This is a simple, natural way of identifying an individual's personality and reflects conscious motives. These traits are relatively consistent general behavior patterns which an individual exhibits in many situations and reveal his adjustment to the environment. Traits are only "relatively permanent" because, even though an individual's personality has an underlying structure of stability and consistency, personality is constantly developing and changing as the individual matures. Traits are only "relatively consistent" because contradictory traits, such as aggression and submission, often exist within the same person and are exhibited at different times. Traits are only general because they are activated by many situations and differing situations can provoke a wide range of responses.

Common traits are those that everyone possesses to some degree. These are traits such as intelligence, gregariousness, introversion, submission and all those related to social adjustment, which everyone has to some degree or another.

Individual traits are specific to one person. In the individual personality there are thought to be cardinal, central and secondary traits.

A cardinal trait is so strong that it colors all of a person's actions and this is the one usually observed and commented on when we give a one-word description of someone.

Central traits are those most typical of the individual. These are the kinds of traits that make us say, "She's always on time, you can set your clock by her," about someone or, "You'll never change her mind on that, she's stubborn as a mule."

Secondary traits are the less prominent ones that are not really typical of an individual that are usually shown only under special circumstances, such as in times of stress. We usually never know how we are going to react to a serious automobile accident until it happens and then sometimes our reaction is surprising. People who never thought of themselves as heroes have been known to pull strangers out of burning cars or chase down a purse snatcher and hold him for the police. Dynamic traits impel the person to activity and stylistic traits indicate a person's manner of behavior.

Because it is known that traits are only "relatively consistent," people have a tremendous capacity to learn and adapt. Someone who has a complex of traits which are indicative of anxiety-related reactions CAN learn to modify them. Understanding that some of these traits exist in one's personality is the first step toward change.

Human Emotional Needs

Every human being has psychological needs. Everyone needs to give and receive love; everyone needs to feel they belong and that they are significant; everyone needs to feel secure; everyone needs to explore and learn; and everyone needs to create--to create something that adds meaning to their lives. Children learn to imitate adults in the satisfaction of these needs. Through a process of trial and error adults taught you what you had to do to receive love and what they would accept from you in return as love. Adults taught you what behavior was acceptable so that you would be included in the family unit and what you could do to receive recognition, both positive and negative. Adults taught you how far you could go in exploring new thoughts or actions and what and how to learn. Adults taught you what you could create and how you could create it. You were disciplined or not, given examples--and through the experience of the consequences of your actions--through trial and error--your needs were met in a negative or positive way.

In the process of having these needs met, the child that you once were developed a set of core beliefs. The child develops:

a SELF-IMAGE--a group of beliefs about personal worth, talents, limitations and place in the scheme of things.

an OTHER-IMAGE--a group of beliefs about others, how others should be treated, what relationships between men and women appear, and what behaviors can be expected from the others met.

a WORLD-IMAGE--a group of beliefs concerning what everyday events mean, just how important they are and some abstract concepts about the meaning of things like patriotism, death, morality and God.

A large portion of the basic elements of each individual's core beliefs were established by the age of seven. Children of this age lack adult reasoning skills, have very little experience, and will accept what adults tell them without question, although many of the beliefs of these adults may be irrational or unrealistic. It is possible to examine these beliefs as an adult and replace the unrealistic ones with realistic ones, but many people never realize they have any need to do so. Most people go throughout their lives basing their actions on a set of beliefs developed before age seven.

Most emotional responses are the result of the way events taking place around you are interpreted. The event takes place, it is interpreted from the perspective of the viewer and his/her core beliefs, there is an emotional reaction to what is being observed and then action is taken based on this reaction.

The weather is an example of how different people react to the same event. A rainy day makes some depressed, inconveniences others, is an excuse to sit by a cozy fire for others, and is viewed by still others, such as farmers, as having major importance for their future.

Part of the mind is constantly evaluating events in terms of how it will impact on your needs and wants. This process is usually taking place automatically and at an unconscious level. Each person's mind has the ability to examine vast amounts of information coming in through all the senses. The mind then makes split-second decisions about whether or not an event is satisfying or threatening. Some actions that took years to learn--such as putting on your clothes and tying your shoes--are now so automatic that they can be done while you think about something else and go about the business of preparing to do something else.

If a need or want is or may be satisfied, there are various positive emotions such as joy, excitement or satisfaction which will be experienced. If a threat is present, the mind will react with fear, anger, irritation, panic, depending on the level of the threat. A loss is experienced as sadness, grief and depression, again, depending upon the nature of the loss. Events are complex, they can satisfy some needs and frustrate others. This is why we often experience mixed emotions.

Emotions that aid us in reaching our goals are self-fulfilling. If they interfere with our ability to find satisfaction in relationships, work or play, they are self-defeating. Emotions that occur for no particular reason can be self-defeating, if they occur at exaggerated levels of intensity, or if they remain for extended periods of time. If an individual becomes enraged over something minor, such as the driver ahead failing to move when the light changes, or broods for days over a casual remark made by a friend, or remains depressed over a minor loss or disappointment, such as a card game or a casual bet, these emotions have become self-defeating. EVERYONE has at least some beliefs and habitual thinking patterns that are irrational or unrealistic.

Perceptual Styles

The solution to a problem is susceptible to many influences outside the limits of the problem itself.

These can include anxiety, anger, and frustration, whether from the problem-solving process itself or from other things that are in your life at that time. If these emotions are present to any noticeable extent, they may interfere with your finding a smooth solution to a problem. Severe anxiety may well impair your problem-solving ability on an exam, and frustration at not being able to work a crossword puzzle may interfere with the right word coming into your head. If you are a very competitive person, the anxiety to succeed might actually increase your efficiency in solving a problem. However, if you become too anxious to succeed, that competitiveness might be defeating because the high level of anxiety could interfere with your efficiency in solving the problem.

Most of us approach a problem or an event with some sort of direction or expectation about the outcome that is the result of prior experience. This is habit, the way you are used to perceiving certain situations. The value or non-value of previous experience is that you have learned certain methods or ways of perception in the past, and you apply them to the present situation. For example, if you find you have conflicting appointments, your traits, your life experience might tell you that it is not polite to break previously arranged meetings. Without that habit, your solution to having more than one appointment might be to go off to keep an appointment to play golf and forget the appointment with Aunt Matilda, who might be waiting for you to take her grocery shopping. Perceptual styles go hand-in-hand with traits to motivate and control behavior. Difficulties arise when there is distorted thinking about what we perceive and how we have been trained as children to handle what we think about what we see.

Selective Remembering

Everyone has a set of memorized "versions of the past" and explanations for why things happened, why you behaved or reacted as you did. Sometimes individuals alter the past--for a variety of reasons: to look more heroic, to appear less stupid, to make the story more colorful, to enlarge on the experience-- there are hundreds of reasons for distorting the past in the retelling. If asked about their childhood, their past work experience, most people tell approximately the same tale each time they are asked. However, this is recalled from a very selective point of view. While this point of view might be accurate, another observer at the same scene could tell it from their point of view, which might also be accurate--but it possibly would be quite a different story. When people tell stories about their childhood, a sibling will often declare, "That's not the way it happened!," and their version of the same occurrence will be very different.

Each of us has a constant dialogue that goes on inside our heads. Much of this self-talk takes the form of sentences repeated over and over. The other part of this internal automatic thinking process concerns the memories each one chooses to recall and the event chosen for mental re-play. An example would be someone who is frustrated over the inability to lose weight. Some of the mental sentences repeated over and over might be, "I've got to go on a diet, I've got to lose this weight." The internal automatic thinking might be of a recent occurrence in the grocery store and the remark made by an insensitive stranger, complete with the put-down answer that would have totally destroyed that rude stranger. If we repeat in our heads the put-down that we might have given, after some time it may become the actual memory of the event.

This kind of constant internal dialogue, selective memories, prepared stories and explanations and the points of view from which they come make up an individual's habitual thinking patterns. The interpretation process that generates the emotions is based almost entirely on a combination of these automatic, habitual thinking patterns and a core belief system.

Unrealistic Thinking

Each of us, at one time or another, uses unrealistic thinking. This thinking creates a distorted view of self, the world, and the place self has in the world--the result of this is often self-defeating behavior. When you experience excessive stress, hunger, fatigue or illness, this type of distorted thinking is particularly apt to occur.

Universal absolutes

This is black-and-white thinking. All-or-nothing thinking is the evaluation of personal qualities and events on rigid should/must rules that force all experience into absolute "good" or "bad" categories.

Events are very rarely completely "good" or completely "bad." When an individual transforms personal evaluations into universal absolutes such as "Everyone SHOULD go to church on Sunday," or "Children MUST eat all their vegetables," or "People OUGHT to give a portion of their salary to charity," this is transforming personal evaluations into rigid rules that apply to everyone in the world.

Black-and-white thinking plays a major role in perfectionist personalities because it is almost impossible for everyone or everything to do or be something absolutely. When the absolute "should," "must," and "ought," cannot be met, mistakes and imperfections are magnified. If the "should," "ought," and "must" is applied to self, any personal failure to meet this standard creates a feeling of inadequacy or lowered self-worth.

Labeling

You meet someone for the first time and observe or talk with him or her for a few minutes. Chances are that even in this short space of time you make judgements about a number of the person's characteristics. We all tend to form impressions quickly on the basis of very little real information. Who hasn't applied a label to themselves or to another person? Everyone has probably said, "She's just too bossy," or "I find him very cold," or "I wish I could be less selfish."

It is very easy to categorize people, places and events with rather simple and usually negative labels. This stereotyping is a process of rigidly categorizing people on the basis of a single characteristic, and then assuming they possess a whole bundle of associated traits and behavior patterns. Many stereotypes are based on prejudice and can be harmful to those they categorize.

Labeling is usually the result of internalizing labels that were used by adults to describe you and/or your siblings when you were a child. As an adult, we tend to use these labels when flaws are noticed or a mistake is made. The difficulty with this is that there is no distinction between the action--such as "bossy," "cold," "selfish"--and the personal worth of the individual.

If we have been identified with a label, we might find it difficult to change that behavior. If we are accustomed to and comfortable with that label and its meaning to us, it is possible to behave negatively rather than move out of the over generalization. The label "cooperative," might make someone reluctant to say "no" to a project they would rather not do. The "macho" label might cause an individual to show bravado in a dangerous situation rather than risk losing the self-image that imparts.

Labeling is inaccurate as it only tells a very little about a person or an event during a very small portion of time. Labels also can generate strong feelings and can cause self-defeating behavior.

Exaggeration

"I'm starving." Obviously, you aren't starving, you only want to go to lunch. "I can't take another minute of this." You can take it for a while longer, you haven't died or gone into convulsions. "I hate math, I'll never get it right." You perhaps do hate math, but if you keep working on the problem, you most likely will solve it. All of these catastrophic type statements are exaggerations. You may be uncomfortable, you may wish you didn't have to take math, you might want to leave your job or an uncomfortable situation, but this kind of exaggeration can become habitual reaction to every day inconvenience.

Another example of exaggerating is habitually turning minor flaws or experiences into major catastrophes. A slow down on the freeway becomes a hair-tearing, sweat-producing experience when repeated to those who wonder why you were late for work.

"I'll never be able to finish this on time, what do they expect of me?" A small task has become a major trauma--and who doesn't remember complaining for fifteen minutes about a task that would take only five to complete? We've all heard small children, when asked to take out the trash, straighten up their room or clear the table, explode, "My friends won't wait, they'll leave without me!"

With exaggerated habitual reactions come exaggerated emotional responses and unnecessary anxiety. Worse, this prevents you from solving the problem and improving the situation.

Exaggerating the achievements or abilities of others creates the illusion that your own achievements or abilities are of lesser value. This type of exaggerating can make you abandon working toward developing a skill or ability since it appears you can never achieve what others have accomplished. "No point in trying to learn a top-spin serve, I'll never be as good as (list any of the top ten at Wimbledon)." Maybe not, but you probably are as good as, or even better than, the players you can realistically expect to encounter.

This kind of exaggeration lowers self-esteem, creates an unwillingness to attempt anything difficult or new, and can produce anxiety and depression.

Discounting

This kind of thinking can play a major role in maintaining a negative belief system about oneself and is very common in individuals who are depressed and anxious. It can become so extreme that even positive experiences are interpreted as negative. "I guess they only gave me the promotion because there wasn't anyone else." "He didn't really mean what he said about my dress, he was only being nice." This deprecation of personal strengths, abilities, and achievements has a constant negative impact on self-esteem.

Mind reading

"He walked right past me without saying 'Hello'; wonder what I did to make him angry?" "Did you see the way she turned away when we came in the door? Guess she was avoiding us again." "She doesn't love me any more. I can tell by the way she got out of the car."

These are assumptions, made on the basis of your own belief system, usually of your own negative self-worth. The expectation that your behavior would make someone angry, that casual acquaintances would want to avoid talking with or greeting you, that you are unlovable, are assumptions made with little or no evidence and no attempt to confirm or deny the assumption.

This type of thinking is a major source of poor interpersonal relationships.

Predicting

Making a prediction about the outcome of some future event can be disastrous if the prediction is usually negative. The rational process is to consider the possibilities before making a prediction. If you say to your self, "There is no point in applying for that job, they probably have hundreds of applicants more qualified than I am," that is predicting without information. What are the possibilities there are lots of other applicants? What are your skills that might make you the best candidate? With few facts, it is just a bad guess.

Logical Errors

Another source of incorrect inferences is the logical error. When a person displays one trait, we often assume that he also has the other traits we customarily associate with that trait. Because someone appears carefree in one situation, we may tend to assume that he is also irresponsible, demanding, and illogical. Or we may assume that someone who seems serious is also pompous and unemotional.

In addition, just as we make logical errors about traits, we also make logical errors about the causes of other's actions, based on our own past experience.

The Road to Panic for Priscilla--
Traits and Styles

Sitting at her desk, as she had done every day for over twelve years, Priscilla realized that she was having difficulty breathing. She leaned back and tried to take some deep breaths and found she couldn't. Hoping that no one would notice, she leaned forward with her arms on her desk and put her head down. At the same time, she realized her heart was pounding. Then Priscilla began to feel very anxious and she tried to get Jennifer's attention, who was sitting at the next desk. When Jennifer looked up she saw that Priscilla's eyes were wide with fright, her mouth was open and she was gasping for breath.

Frightened herself, Jennifer hurried over. "What's wrong, what's wrong?"

Priscilla could only point to her throat because she now felt as if she were choking. Jennifer began to slap her on the back and suddenly Priscilla took a big deep breath and waved her off. "I'm OK now, must have gotten a peanut stuck in my throat," she lied.

Frightened and shaken, Priscilla assumed that there was some physical reason for this experience and made an appointment with her doctor. After a thorough examination of her throat, lungs and chest, Priscilla's doctor pronounced her OK and said, "Maybe you've just been working too hard, why don't you take a little vacation, get some rest and relaxation."

Being told that she was fine was not good news to Priscilla. She KNEW that there was definitely something wrong. Raised in a structured religious home, Priscilla possessed some of the traits that are typical of individuals who go on to have panic attacks. She had a very great need to appear to be in control of the situation at all times, to get the approval of her peers and to avoid embarrassing herself in public. She assumed that others would think she was "weak" and began to imagine what her co-workers would say if it should happen again. Now she really began to worry that this would happen again and she would appear foolish in the

eyes of her co-workers, an almost unbearable thought. Priscilla never even considered
that the people she had worked beside for
twelve years might care about her health or
have genuine concern for her well-being. She
began to see this as a catastrophe and spent
some time telling herself that she absolutely
"must not" have this embarrassment again.

This worry caused Priscilla to become
aware of all sorts of little internal sensations. She began to lie awake at night and
concentrate on listening to her heartbeat and
her breathing. What if she would be unable
to breathe in church? What if she would
have to put her head down in some important meeting at work? "What if. . .what if. . . ."
and Priscilla was on the road to negative
anticipation and panic attack.

Priscilla now began to worry endlessly.
Lack of sleep and the intrusion of the "what
if" thinking led her to focus on physical sensations she had ignored in the past. As she
thought about the situations where this could
be embarrassing for her, her heart would
start to pound and her breathing rate would
increase. She began to "squirrel cage" some
thoughts; that is, circle them around and

around without any solution. "I can't let this happen again. I have to stay in control of myself." Priscilla's reaction to this perfectly normal response to her negative thinking caused a fight-or-flight response and increased the physical reactions she was experiencing. With this came the fear, fear that this was all happening again and of course, even stronger fight-or-flight physical sensations. The anxiety/panic cycle escalated and Priscilla talked herself into a self-generated panic attack.

Chapter 6
The Biology--
Causes or Effects?

THE COMPLEX RESPONSE WITH BRAIN CHEMICALS that takes place within every individual to thoughts about the environment is meant to keep us safe. By interpreting what we see and hear, we can provide ourselves with information about what is threatening and what is not threatening in the present environment. Once we have interpreted the possibility of danger, we can take proper action to ensure safety.

We see a car speeding toward us as we are about to cross the street. Our brain sends a message via chemical messengers to the muscles. "Jump back-- out of the way of danger." Our muscles respond immediately and we are back on the curb and out of harm's way. For the average person there are a few moments of increased heart rate, increased intake of oxygen, perhaps a few moments of shaky muscles and then it is over.

For the individual prone to high anxiety there is an exaggerated fight-or-flight response to the situation, adrenaline pours out into the bloodstream, and one is left shaking on the curb, terrified.

For the individual prone to high anxiety there may not need to be a speeding car at all. This person responds more intensely to environmental stimuli such as noise, odors, medications and variations in temperature. For individuals with both the biological factor and the high anxiety traits, plus a distorted perceptual style, a stressful event in their lives (such as a death in the family, a new job, a new baby in the family, conflict with a supervisor) can cause the person to exaggerate the stress that normally accompanies these events. A high anxiety individual also tends to ignore the physical needs of their own body. This combination of a stressed physical structure and excessive mental stress now interacts with the inherited biological factor and produces an exaggerated fight-or-flight response.

Hyperventilation

Breathing more rapidly or deeply than is necessary is known as hyperventilation. This process may produce many of the characteristic symptoms of anxiety and possibly is the trigger for the symptoms of panic. For many, their first panic attack was actually a hyperventilation episode. For others, hyperventilation accompanies the panic attack and accounts for many of the symptoms. It is possible that many individuals have BOTH a biological factor coupled with the tendency to hyperventilate.

Dr. Donald Klein, professor of psychiatry at Columbia University says, "It may be a simple case of some faulty wiring--a defect in the way this person's brain warns against suffocation." Along with assorted other alarms, the human brain has a warning system that fires whenever the amount of carbon dioxide in the blood becomes too high--a sure sign of oxygen deprivation.

In some people, the system is overly sensitive and fires spontaneously at the slightest increase in blood CO2. This false alarm then sets off a cascade of events that culminate in panic attack. Just before the attack, the victim is overwhelmed by feelings of suffocation and tries to compensate by breathing deeply. But it is too late, and the heavy breathing can't alleviate the feeling of suffocation.

"The brain says, 'let's get out of here'," observes Klein. People having panic attacks often run to the window and throw it open, or run outside. They are trying to get some air in."

Proof that a suffocation monitor exists, he says, lies in infants who are born without one, those with the defect known as Ondine's curse (sleep-induced apnea). Suffocation is particularly aversive to the human brain, and most infants cry instinctively whenever their noses are held--they have a minor panic reaction. But children with Ondine's calmly suffocate without any response at all.

Overbreathing, or hyperventilation, occurs when an individual breathes more rapidly or more deeply, or a combination of both, than is necessary to meet the demands of the body for oxygen and the removal of the waste product, carbon dioxide.

Breathing in this excessive manner causes the blood level of carbon dioxide to drop by as much as fifty percent in as little as thirty seconds. Because we think of carbon dioxide as a waste product, as many of us were taught in elementary school, we often "force the bad air out and the good air in" when we are in a stressful situation. It is not unusual for someone who is upset or nervous to be told, "Take a deep breath." This is fine for the individual who has restricted their breathing or is holding their breath because of an anxiety-provoking situation.

However, carbon dioxide has a secondary function within the mechanisms of the body. It maintains the pH level of the blood. When we over-breathe we elevate the pH levels in nerve cells, making them more responsive. This INITIATES a chain reaction of activity in the body. It takes only a tiny amount of change in the pH level to bring about the effects of increased heart rate, constriction of blood vessels, and a rise again in pH levels, a cycle which re-initiates the body's fight-or-flight response.

This response will develop in less than a minute

and most people do not associate the symptoms with over-breathing; they usually respond to the other bodily symptoms such as a pounding heart, difficulty swallowing, sweating, fatigue, shaking or numbness and tingling of the hands or feet as being caused by some external stimuli.

During hyperventilation the levels of carbon dioxide can become TOO LOW, resulting in a condition known as respiratory alkalosis. Symptoms of alkalosis include light-headedness, dizziness, and numbness.

Most of us have seen someone being given a paper bag to breathe into when they are upset--this is based on the very logical concept that the re-breathing of the carbon dioxide will act on the body's pH balance, returning it to its proper level quickly, ending the fight-or-flight symptoms. BUT FOR PANIC DISORDER PATIENTS, BREATHING INTO A PAPER BAG MAY BE THE WORST THING TO DO.

Hyperventilation and panic disorder do have a great many similarities:

Both often occur after muscular exertion, just upon waking or falling to sleep.

Both experience similar physiological changes.

Both precipitate symptoms of hyperventilation (rapid breathing, pounding heart, dizziness, feelings of being suffocated, trembling, etc.).

A very large number of people experience both panic disorder and frequent hyperventilation

It is obvious that hyperventilation and panic disorder are very closely related conditions.

Researchers studying both conditions have observed that hyperventilation may serve as a trigger for a panic attack. In two differing studies, patients were intentionally hyperventilated under controlled conditions. In one study, 60 percent of the patients experienced panic symptoms; in the second study, 90 percent of the subjects reported experiencing symptoms of panic.

If the opposite is true, that panic causes hyperventilation, then hyperventilation should *always* result in panic. Studies have shown that this doesn't occur. But what does create panic is the inhalation of carbon dioxide.

What does the difference mean? One explanation is that hyperventilation itself, where extra oxygen is taken in, doesn't always alter the blood pH. Panic disorder patients may have found that sufficient hyperventilation is a means of keeping blood levels of carbon dioxide low. If carbon dioxide is actually the cause of panic, then some panic patients become chronic hyperventilators in order to keep their carbon dioxide levels low enough to avoid the symptoms of the disorder.

For this reason, the cure for hyperventilation, of re-breathing in a paper bag, which for ordinary individuals would rebalance the blood pH, may result in triggering a panic attack in chronic hyperventilators by raising their blood level of carbon dioxide, rather than lowering it.

In controlled studies, carbon dioxide inhalation and sodium lactate infusion have been shown to be almost equally effective in provoking panic attacks in panic-prone individuals.

Breathing Patterns

Humans use two basic breathing patterns. Upper-chest or thoracic-breathing lifts the chest upward and outward, and the breathing is shallow and rapid. Relaxed or diaphragmatic breathing is deeper and slower. As the lower portions of the lungs are filled with air, they push down on the diaphragm and cause the abdomen to protrude.

Upper-chest breathing is used during strenuous exercise in order to provide the active body with the large amounts of oxygen needed to sustain the vigorous activity.

Relaxed breathing or diaphragmatic breathing is more normal breathing. This type of breathing is used during every day activities such as working at your desk or reading.

During the day most people will alternate between upper-chest breathing and relaxed breathing, as their bodily requirements dictate.

Many individuals with anxiety related difficulties unconsciously adopt upper-chest breathing as their primary breathing method. Others quickly convert to upper-chest breathing as soon as they become anxious. Upper-chest breathing is the logical response to any threatening situation. It is triggered by the adrenaline or fight-or-flight response and it prepares the body for the strenuous activity of fighting or running from danger.

Someone who habitually uses the upper-chest breathing may feel continually threatened by normal every day situations and be completely unaware that this breathing pattern has become habitual.

Mouth breathing can also cause hyperventilation. Individuals who suffer from allergies, asthma or other obstructive disorders are often forced to breathe in this manner because of difficulty in breathing through the nose. When excited, stressed or even during mild exercise, mouth-breathers may experience symptoms of hyperventilation.

Breath-holding is another form of hyperventilation. Some people, when experiencing anxiety, will hold their breath in anticipation of the unpleasant event. The result of breath-holding is a need to increase oxygen intake to offset the oxygen deficit caused during the momentary breath-holding. The result will be a drop in the carbon dioxide levels and the cycle of symptoms of hyperventilation.

The panic or anxiety attack that seems to come "out of the blue" can be explained by any one of these causes of hyperventilation. It only needs a very minor degree of hyperventilation to trigger the effects of an increased heart rate, constriction of the blood vessels, and a rise in the pH level of the blood. The symptoms these reactions produce are then noticeable and they can trigger the anxiety/panic cycle.

The Chemistry of Sodium Lactate and Carbon Dioxide

Researchers observed that individuals who experienced panic or anxiety found that their conditions worsened after vigorous exercise. Upon examination of blood test results, it was found that these people had higher levels of blood lactate following exercise, while normal individuals' levels of lactate were significantly lower.

In controlled studies, researchers infused enough lactate into subjects to reach the same levels that are produced by strenuous exercise. Panic disorder patients had panic attacks from the infusion, while the normal subjects did not.

The similarities between the panic-producing properties of sodium lactate and carbon dioxide led researchers to study the underlying biological mechanism shared by both of these substances.

Sodium lactate is broken down and oxidized into bicarbonate ions. This is a very normal process that the body uses to rid itself of waste products. Bicarbonate ions cannot enter the brain as they are not allowed to cross the blood-brain barrier, a very wonderful barrier that protects the brain from all kinds of negative factors that could damage this very central source of life. So, these bicarbonate ions circulate around in the blood stream, eventually joining hydrogen ions to form carbonic acid. This carbonic acid will eventually break down into our panic disorder-causing substance, carbon dioxide, which is ordinarily excreted by exhalation. In this form, carbon dioxide can now enter the brain, where it can collect at the locus ceruleus and produce panic attacks in panic-prone individuals, just as inhaled carbon dioxide does.

This concentration of carbon dioxide in the brain then may cause the locus ceruleus to increase its activity, fire more neurotransmitters in response to this "suffocation alarm" in those sensitive to its effects.

The Panic Valve

Mitral valve prolapse has been found to occur more frequently in people who have panic attacks. When the mitral valve fails to operate properly, blood flows in the wrong direction in the cardiac area.

Panic attacks in individuals with mitral valve prolapse were reported by University of Chicago investigators and University of Michigan physicians in the *New England Journal of Medicine*. Investigators believe that the condition is passed on from mother to child during the sixth week of fetal development.

The "out of the blue" panic attack can be experienced by those who have this mitral valve prolapse condition. In the diagnostic criteria for panic disorder as listed in *The Diagnostic and Statistical Manual of Mental Disorders* of the American Psychiatric Association, it is noted that mitral valve prolapse may be an associated condition. Because one of the symptoms of mitral valve prolapse is often a "skipped" beat of the heart or some other internal symptom that may be noticed, often for the first time, this can be the trigger for a panic attack. The type of internalization associated with the anxiety/panic cycle can cause the individual to become very sensitive to any internal sensation. If symptoms of hyperventilation or panic usually follow such an internal sensation, then that will become recognized as a "sign" that a dreaded anxiety attack is about to happen.

Does Alcohol Abuse = Panic Disorder?

The relationship between substance abuse and anxiety disorders appears to be a strong one.

Because alcohol provides rapid relief from the symptoms of panic, as many as 10-20 percent of panic disorder victims have drinking problems at some stage during their illness.

It is estimated that one third of alcoholics have panic disorder or social phobias BEFORE they begin using alcohol to alleviate their symptoms.

Since many people with anxiety-related problems develop substance abuse problems as a result of an attempt to calm their anxiety through the use of alcohol and tranquilizers, it is often necessary to first treat the substance abuse before any progress can be made in the treatment of anxiety-related disorders.

All Stressed Out

Stress is anything that triggers your fight-or-flight or adrenaline response. The effects of stress can be both positive and negative. Positive stress is the excitement an experienced performer feels just before a performance. In this case, the adrenaline helps improve the performance.

Negative stress can be short-term (such as the fear, pressure, and the need for quick decisions when the driver in the car in front of you suddenly slams on his or her brakes), or long-term (such as the stress you might feel in a complex, high pressure job). Too much stress, especially over a long period of time, can drain energy, cause undue wear and tear on the body, and make an individual vulnerable to illness, premature aging and psychological breakdown. Photographs of presidents when they entered office and when they left, a matter of only four years in some cases, provide a vivid example of the toll a high-stress job can take on the body and appearance.

We can divide stress into two major types: physical stress and psychological stress. Physical stress is created by demands on the body such as those caused by accidents, illness, lack of sleep, chemical toxins, a demanding work schedule, or prolonged psychological stress. Psychological stress is created by mental or emotional demands on the body. Psychological stress can be simply the result of physical stress. However, psychological stress is more often caused by mental or emotional demands from your personal beliefs, family, work or friends. Examples of psychological stress are:

Pressure

An internal or external demand to complete an activity either within a limited amount of time or in a specific manner. (Meeting a deadline or creating something that must meet the employer's criteria).

Frustration

What is wanted to meet either physical or psychological needs or desires is blocked. (A date with someone interesting is repeatedly refused. The family has grown but there are insufficient funds to purchase a larger home.)

Conflict

The need to make a choice. (A job offer in a distant city. It pays more but housing is much more expensive there. You would be willing to move for a promotion but your partner isn't.)

Anxiety

A response to a perceived threat.

Physical symptoms of anxiety are generated when any of the stressors trigger the adrenaline response. The body responds to any thought as though the thought concerns an event which is occurring NOW. It does not matter whether the thought is about the past, present or the future. Dwelling on past embarrassments--something that happened in high school where the entire class laughed, even though the event took place years ago. Thinking about "what ifs" that might happen in the future--What if the project being presented tomorrow is rejected?

A vivid thought accompanied by strong emotion about a past negative experience or a possible future problem can trigger the adrenaline response. Fight-or-flight is in operation even though there is not a NOW event.

Individuals who experience the prolonged stress of severe anxiety usually have beliefs, attitudes and habitual thinking patterns which perpetuate the stress. How often is the embarrassing situation that took place years ago in the person's thoughts, as compared to the event in the past which was very pleasurable, such as an award or a compliment? How often is the expectation that work will be rewarded with praise and promotion rather than embarrassment or disappointment?

The negative anticipation of the consequences of events which have yet to take place and the constant review of negative past events are common habitual thinking patterns. Habitual thinking patterns with WHAT IFS that are negative, rather than positive, can seriously contribute to severe anxiety on a daily basis.

Many studies have found an unusually high incidence of stressful life events in the months preceding first panic attacks. One study reported that 90 percent of first panic attacks were preceded by major stressors. These life stressors were most likely to be death or serious illness of a close relative or friend, or serious illness of or danger to the self.

However, stress has been shown to be a precursor to a number of other conditions beside anxiety disorders. Cardiovascular disease, multiple sclerosis, diabetes, back pain, headaches, insomnia, depression are just some of the conditions preceded by major stress. It would seem obvious that stress is very wearing on the emotions and on the immune system. There is a theory that the "Achilles heel" of each individual determines just which body system will fail first due to stress.

However, not everyone develops panic attacks after a major life stress. Researchers have known for many years that the body, when under certain types of stress, especially physical stress, undergoes neuroendocrine changes, specifically in the hypothalamus, the pituitary, and the adrenal glands. These structures secrete increased levels of the hormones ACTH and cortisol during physical stress. Some researchers have suggested that since the physical symptoms of a panic attack resemble the symptoms of physical stress, changes in hormonal levels might occur in panic attacks; thus, panic attacks might be a consequence of changes in the level of hormones.

Numerous studies designed to measure the hormone levels of panic patients have not found significantly higher levels of hormonal activity. This failure to demonstrate that elevated hormonal levels occur during panic attacks tends to support the theory that stress merely weakens the Achilles heel portion of the system and then that will allow the panic tendency to exert its influence.

The Nightmare

Many individuals report that they frequently have panic attacks during sleep and for that reason, find themselves reluctant to go to bed at night.

Some studies indicate that when nighttime panic occurs, it is almost always during the non-rapid-eye-movement (non-REM) periods of sleep. In the non-REM sleep periods, dreaming does not take place, and sleep is not as deep and refreshing as in the REM sleep.

Researchers at Children's Hospital Medical Center found that, unlike adults, infants begin REM as soon as they fall asleep. This active cycle alternates with deep sleep every forty-five minutes. Babies who were given tryptophan, the amino acid precursor of serotonin, increased their active sleep or REM sleep. This research is thought to have some implications for the nighttime panic attacks of adults.

If serotonin levels can be raised, REM sleep can be increased, therefore decreasing the non-REM periods of sleep, when the nighttime panic appears to take place.

The fact that panic attacks occur during the non-dreaming state also gives credibility to the belief that there is a biological basis for panic attacks.

The Freudian Thinking

A team of Pittsburgh and New York psychiatrists admits that some biological predisposition for panic attacks does exist. But, they maintain, panic attacks don't happen in the absence of certain kinds of early experience and psychic conflict.

Resurrecting the theories of Sigmund Freud, they insist that both biology and early experience conspire to cause panic. In their neo-Freudian model, innate temperament, psychodynamics, parental behavior, and objective and subjective experience all play a role.

According to this theory, people with the disorder are born with a neurophysiological irritability that shows itself as early fearfulness. As children, they typically fear new or unfamiliar situations. Their parents, perhaps anxious or prone to panic them- selves, fail to ease the way they fit with the world and wind up exacerbating the child's fearful nature.

The child feels threatened and suffocated by par- ents' behavior but at the same time becomes overly dependent on them. In adolescence, the child be- comes very complaisant and eager to please, but at the same time resentful of authority.

Now the steep slide towards the first panic at- tack begins. At some point in early adulthood, some- thing happens, usually involving a powerful other or figure of authority, to make the future sufferer ex- tremely angry or upset. Already predisposed toward fear, she becomes frightened at her intense negative emotions. Anger leads to a physical response--heavy heartbeat, sweating, anxiety--and this triggers a fight- or-flight reaction in the brain.

These doctors feel this first attack begins a vi- cious cycle. Fear of another panic attack leads to more psychological vulnerability, which leads to more fear that may result in another panic attack. In some sufferers, the attacks may occur over a brief period of time and then never reappear. In others, the end- less chain of fear and panic may go on for years, virtually destroying the ability to function normally, according to Katherine Shear, professor of psychia- try at the University of Pittsburgh, and colleagues.

The study, which involved only nine patients, was an outgrowth of interviews with these nine, published reports of psychological characteristics of panic patients, and data from animal and infant research on temperament. All patients described themselves as shy and nervous children, and their parents as suffocating, critical, and demanding. All reported later problems with overdependency and fear of authority. And all described stressful incidents just before the onset of their first panic attack.

Those Raging Hormones

Hormones are substances that travel through the bloodstream to organs or tissues where they exert a specific effect on the activities of those body parts.

Examples are the thyroid hormones, growth hormones, the corticosteroids and the catecholamines. A hormone can also be a neurotransmitter when it sends a chemical message. Neurotransmitters such as norepinephrine, epinephrine, dopamine and serotonin are classified as catecholamine neurotransmitter hormones (chemical messengers that affect the nervous system).

Researchers have found that individuals with anxiety disorders have different levels of circulating hormones than what is considered normal levels in most other people. In the majority of cases, these individuals have elevated levels of hormones most of the time. In fact, they have unusually high levels of some of these particular neurotransmitter hormones. Some of these neurotransmitter hormones have anxiety-provoking properties; some have calming properties.

The neurotransmitters control our behavior by reacting on specific receptors in the brain. It is possible that individuals who have panic attacks have a "hair trigger" response with an elevated level of the anxiety-provoking hormones circulating in their bloodstream.

It is important that we get the proper precursors in our diet to manufacture neurotransmitters.

And now, the tricky part of understanding some of this biochemistry. It is not necessary to read this section. If you want to, you can skip to the part that tells what to do about the problems with your biochemistry. But for those who want to understand the why, read on.

The Amino Acid Inhibitors

Amino acids are the building blocks of proteins. There are nine essential amino acids required to make proteins and they are introduced into the human body through the diet. There are eleven more amino acids that are made by the body and are necessary for a variety of functions. Certain neurons in the nervous system inhibit nerve impulses by releasing specific molecules called inhibitory transmitters. An inhibitory neuron damps or eliminates the firing of its target cells. One such amino acid is gamma aminobutyric acid or GABA. Neurons secrete GABA and prevent uncontrolled neural firing, acting as a brake on the entire nervous system. This gamma aminobutyric acid inhibitory transmitter (GABA) has receptor sites in the brain's limbic system, an area of the brain known to influence a wide range of behavior, including pleasure, anger and fear. This system is the emotional alarm system. It is activated by stress and sends out messages of anxiety, fear, dread, and anger.

Drugs such as Valium, Librium and Ativan act upon these receptor sites, calming anxiety and stress reactions. With sufficient GABA (natures' inhibitory agent for these receptors) filling the receptor sites, the limbic system would be prevented from overwhelming the cortex of the brain with anxiety messages.

Because of the high level of excitory hormones usually circulating in the blood of those who are anxiety-prone, it is thought that the biochemical requirements for inhibitory neurotransmitter amino acids in the nervous systems of anxiety-prone individuals are vastly increased. It is possible that there is an elevated requirement for GABA in those who experience prolonged periods of stress, anxiety and/or depression. But remember, GABA is secreted by internal cells and if we have a little biochemical unbalance, then these cells may not be producing proper amounts of GABA. However, it is possible to supplement GABA, and how that can be done will be explained in the chapter on Solutions (Chapter 12).

The Serotonin Connection

One of the essential amino acids is tryptophan, which is necessary to maintain the body in protein balance. Tryptophan is available in the diet from milk and milk products. Perhaps you might remember a time in childhood when you were given a glass of warm milk to help you sleep. Your parents probably did not understand the biochemistry, but they knew that warm milk was effective as a sleep-inducing agent. It was the amino acid tryptophan that provided the necessary amino acid to make another neurotransmitter known as serotonin. This neurotransmitter acted in a complex manner to help you go to sleep. Serotonin is a natural antidepressant that can decrease anxiety, tension and anger while increasing concentration. Its action can be artificially duplicated with anti-depressant drugs. In nature, tryptophan is a precursor of this neurotransmitter.

Serotonin is unique among neurotransmitters. It is one of several chemicals that transmit impulses between neurons, but it does not have receptors localized in a few specific brain regions. Instead, nerve cells tipped with serotonin-sensitive binding sites cluster deep within the brain stem and send neuronal tentacles throughout the brain, so that their uptake and release of serotonin ultimately affects much of a person's mental life. Tryptophan is one of the few substances capable of passing the blood-brain barrier.

Researchers at the Veterans Administration Medical Center in New York have found that male alcoholics whose heavy drinking began before age twenty are more prone to depression and violent behavior than other alcoholic men. Their report in the *Archives of General Psychiatry* suggests that alcoholics who start excessive drinking early may be deficient in serotonin, because that brain chemical is tied to mood and aggression.

Researchers at the National Institute on Alcohol Abuse and Alcoholism have also demonstrated a connection between impulsive murders committed by convicted males and chronically low levels of a serotonin breakdown product. They also found abnormally low levels of this breakdown product in a study of violent offenders and impulsive arsonists. That does not mean that all individuals with low levels of serotonin will become criminals, it just points out that low levels of this neurotransmitter can cause brain chemical imbalances that can lead to further problems, depending upon the predisposing personality of the individual.

Some readers may recall that L-tryptophan (an artificially produced form of the chemical) used to be available in any health food store as a "natural" remedy for insomnia, premenstrual syndrome and depression, and that it was removed from the market by the Food and Drug Administration the 1980s. The reason for its recall was that a number of people died and hundreds suffered from a disease known as eosinophilia-myalgia syndrome. This disease was eventually linked to the use of L-tryptophan. The causative agent in this disease was then linked to the genetically engineered L-tryptophan manufactured by the Japanese firm Showa Denko, which was supplying about 40 percent of the U.S. tryptophan market at that time.

Although it is now thought by most researchers that the timing of the mysterious outbreak of eosinophilia-myalgia syndrome was linked to the L-tryptophan batches manufactured with a new strain of bacillus called Strain V. by Showa Denko, the Japanese manufacturing firm, L-tryptophan has never been returned to the marketplace.

However, tryptophan, the precursor to serotonin, is readily available through an intake of dairy products such as milk, cottage cheese and yogurt.

Worried to Death

Studies at Rush Presbyterian-St. Luke's Medical Center in Chicago suggest that the unbearable level of anxiety known as a panic attack is a major risk factor for suicide. In a study of nearly 1,000 psychiatric patients, those most likely to commit suicide suffered from a combination of depression and anxiety, a form of which includes panic disorder.

A further study at New York City's Columbia University found that panic attacks and panic disorder are linked to a strong and largely unappreciated risk of contemplating and attempting suicide. In a study of 18,000 adults, the researchers found that 1 in 5 people with panic disorder had attempted suicide, compared to about 1 in 8 with panic attacks, 1 in 16 with other psychiatric disorders, and 1 in 100 with no disorder.

In national samples many panic disorder sufferers have been found to be unaware that any treatment exists for their condition, thus stoking their feelings of demoralization and helplessness that contributes to suicidal thoughts and actions.

It is frightening to realize that this intense fear of fear can become so unbearable that some individuals will not only see the situation as hopeless, but seek such a drastic solution as ending their lives to stop the pain.

Such statistics are a strong testimonial to the extreme emotional and physical pain caused by panic attacks, but they also point out the strength and determination of the majority of those who suffer from panic attacks and do not take their own lives.

In a study conducted by the National Institute of Mental Health, it was found that imbalances of the neurotransmitter serotonin were associated with suicide, depression and violence. A study at the University of Helsinki in Finland demonstrated that there was a connection among violence and suicide attempts, aggression and impulsive murders, and chronically low levels of serotonin.

If your panic attacks are so severe that you have contemplated suicide, it is time to get outside intervention NOW--while you learn what you can do to control and end your symptoms. Do not despair, THERE IS HELP FOR YOU.

The family and friends of those who suffer from panic disorder should be alert to the suicidal potential. Talking about "ending it all," making statements about possible suicide methods; giving away precious objects and belongings to friends and family; increased substance abuse; disturbances in patterns

of daily behavior such as loss of appetite, sleeplessness, isolation and withdrawal, are all suicide clues.
Keep in mind that most suicidal threats are essentially "cries for help" and they can provide a useful
framework for encouraging the sufferer to get help.

Barbara's Thoughts of Suicide

Ten years ago, Barbara suffered her first
panic attack while sitting at her desk during
a normal work day. That first attack changed
her life forever and almost ended it.

"Since that day, I've been overwhelmed
by a feeling of sudden death hundreds of
times," says 32-year old Barbara.

"In the middle of an ordinary day I would
be struck numb by fear, for no reason at all.
I would scream, just as if I were falling from
the top of a skyscraper, expecting to hit the
ground any second. I would stand there,
fixed on the spot, with my heart hammering
so fast I thought it would explode. It didn't
take many of these episodes for those who
worked with me to decide I was more than
a little crazy." Barbara laughed, "It all sounds
so silly now, but I soon was without work,
unable to work, and this finally left me re-
treating from the entire world.

"I would be in the supermarket. I would begin shaking like a leaf in a windstorm and a lump would come into my throat so big that breathing was impossible, I would think that I was going to choke to death. I would abandon my cart in the middle of the store and run outside to try to get some air. Then I would be so embarrassed that I couldn't go back into the store, I would just go home without any groceries."

After that first attack, Barbara's episodes become more frequent. Doctors couldn't pinpoint the problem. "I was diagnosed with everything from ear ailments to 'kookiness.'

"I just stayed at home with my mother and as time went by I thought, 'Why suffer thinking that this was it, I am going to die from this?' I decided that I was not going to suffer like this any longer, I was going to end it for once and for all."

Fortunately for Barbara, her mother recognized some of the signs of suicidal ideation and she got emergency treatment. Finally, one doctor made a correct diagnosis--Barbara was suffering from panic disorder.

"I had hope. I wasn't crazy after all!"

In addition to receiving medication,

advice on limiting caffeine and changing her diet, Barbara got treatment from a therapist who specialized in treating panic disorder with cognitive therapy. Within months, Barbara was back in control of her life.

"It is so difficult to believe now. It only took months. I got medication, emotional support. I learned about chemicals such as caffeine, the part diet played in the disorder and I began to work with my therapist on how I view the world. I learned that I always saw everything as a catastrophe, a disaster and that was very unrealistic. It took some work to change my outlook but gradually, I began to see that I was, in some ways, my own worst enemy. My only regret now is that it took years, years of my life when I was only existing, not living."

Barbara is employed again and gives some of her time to a panic disorder support group to help other sufferers. "It makes me feel so good to be able to give some aid to others by helping them short-circuit this disease--to get on with their lives and see there is something they can do about it, to regain control."

PART III

What Can I Do About It?

Chapter 7
Prisoners of Panic
Looking for a Reprieve

IF

You feel anxious and/or have panic attacks, phobias or some other kind of anxiety.

You are currently being treated for an anxiety problem or panic attacks.

You are considering seeking treatment for anxiety or panic attacks.

You are wondering what kind of treatment to seek for your anxiety or panic attacks.

Someone in your family or a friend suffers from anxiety or panic attacks.

You have looked for years for some kind of answer, have almost given up hope because you think your symptoms are the result of some kind of weakness of character or lack of self-control.

You have been told that you exaggerate or that you should just "get on with your life." -

Are feeling desperate and hopeless.

AND

>   You don't know or aren't sure just what to do next.

KNOW

>   Panic attacks and anxiety disorders are treatable.

YOU CAN LEARN TO TAKE CHARGE. There are SOLUTIONS and they are all things that you can control.

FIRST

>   Have a complete medical examination to see if there is any hidden medical problem that could be causing your symptoms.

>   If you have some physical condition--treat that condition first. That may be the end of your symptoms.

>   It is possible to have a physical condition AND panic disorder, so you need to know about the medical component before you can make any sensible decisions about what to do next to get better.

SECOND

>   Most people experience traumatic life events. Some individuals develop panic disorder and others do not. The difference appears to be the combination of some slight abnormality in brain

chemistry plus the traits that can be considered high-anxiety. Consider your family of origin and how you were socialized. Take a good look at your personality. If you feel you have any of the high-anxiety personality traits, and they are so extreme that they could be contributing to your anxiety, then you may need to seek the assistance of a therapist to work on these aspects of your personality. It may take work in this area to alter how you view the world and how you respond to your environment.

THIRD

Accept the possibility that there could be a genetic/biological basis for your difficulty. If this is a possibility, consider that you may have to alter some of your ways of day-to-day living that impact on this "hair trigger" biochemistry, such as diet, alcohol use and exercise.

It is possible that the solution for you can be as simple as a minor life-style change.

FOURTH

Learn what YOU can do to change the things in your condition that contribute to anxiety.

Then--TAKE ACTION!!

First Aid

When you are hit by a panic attack, your first reaction is to tense up, run outside, trying to get more air and become more and more frantic. The more tense your muscles--the more intense the fear.

Plan what you will do when you have another panic attack before you have one. Although you do not know where you will be, you need to have a first aid plan for yourself.

1. Stop. Do not run. Sit down, if possible. Take several deep abdominal breaths and exhale slowly.

2. Remain aware that the symptoms will pass. Try to take yourself to a safe place you have previously created in your mind that you have created when you have practiced relaxing. Consciously relax your hands and your neck.

3. When your symptoms have gone, take a few minutes alone and go over what may have caused the attack to happen at this moment in your life. Have you been neglecting your health? How is your diet? Have you been drinking caffeine, eating sugary foods? The panic attack may be a signal from your body that it is time to take care of it. Listen to the message.

You have gone to the doctor. You've got a diagnosis.

But when you have such a diagnosis as panic disorder, or phobia, it essential that you understand the diagnosis and its ramifications. Understandably, many individuals are defensive about receiving what they perceive as being a "psychiatric" diagnosis. If you can accept that the disorder stems from a malfunction of central nervous system receptors then you are on your way to a cure, control and an END TO PANIC ATTACKS. Panic disorder is a very treatable condition. The rewards are worth the effort, especially if your intervention is early enough to prevent complications--depression, alcohol abuse and agoraphobia--which can be more difficult to treat than the underlying disorder. It is reassuring to know that the condition is fairly common and that there are medications which can bring the symptoms under control. It is also reassuring to know that other people experience similar attacks, that you are not going to die during an attack, and that you are not losing your mind.

For someone who has experienced only a few attacks, sometimes education and reassurance are enough to forestall further episodes.

The symptoms are physical and the first line of treatment may be a medication and/or medications which have an anti-panic effect and help control the uncomfortable and often disturbing physical manifestations. Although medication is often the first most desirable early therapeutic step, you may resist drug therapy for a number of reasons. Individuals with this condition are often obsessed with maintaining control, and they perceive taking medicine as a loss of control. In addition, the fears may become so generalized that you may be wary of anything unfamiliar, including a new medication.

The treatment of panic disorder is analogous to the treatment of other complex, chronic conditions such as asthma, diabetes, or hypertension: if the disorder goes untreated, there is a ripple effect of secondary complications. The targets of panic disorder therapy are the metabolic core of the disorder, and the psychosocial problems that complicate the condition.

The goal of drug treatment is to block the unexpected attacks of symptoms. Knowing that the attacks are blocked may be helpful in enabling you to go on with other aspects of panic disorder therapy.

The Drugs

There are three main groups of drugs used to treat anxiety-related problems.

Tricyclic antidepressants such as imipramine (Tofranil), desipramine (Norpramine), nortriptyline

(Pamelor), and amitriptyline (Elavil).

Monamine oxidase inhibitors (the MAOI's are another class of antidepressants) such as phenelzine (Nardil), isocarboxizid (Marplan), and tranycypromine (Parnate).

Benzodiazepines such as alprazolam (Xanax), clonazepam (Klonopin), lorazepan (Ativan), and diazepam (Valium).

Xanax is the most-prescribed drug for panic disorder in America. In 1990 it became the only drug ever approved by the Food and Drug Administration for the treatment of panic disorder. It is the country's largest selling psychiatric drug and the fifth most frequently prescribed drug in the United States. Xanax works by binding at stereo specific receptors at several sites within the central nervous system. It is indicated for the management of anxiety disorders or the short-term relief of the symptoms of anxiety. It should be noted that the indication is for short-term relief, as these classes of drugs are highly addictive.

Other classes of drugs that are sometimes used include the beta-blockers such as propranolol (Inderal) or atenolol (Tenormin), a monoamine oxidase inhibitor (MAIO) phenelzine (Nardil), and non-benzodiazepine tranquilizers such as buspirone (Buspar). These medications can lower the number of beta-receptors in the brain, and taken with others which prevent the remaining receptors from being stimulated, have relieved panic attacks and reduced their frequency in a large number of patients.

The Anxiety Disorders Association of America will provide a pamphlet called "The Consumer's Guide to Medication for Panic Disorder" which describes the various medications used with anxiety-related problems along with how they are used.

NONE--that is NONE--of these medications will prevent panic attacks completely but they will reduce the over-all level of anxiety. Sometimes, however, it is necessary to go through a trial-and-error period until the right medication and correct dosage are found. For many sufferers, medication helps reduce not only the number of attacks but their intensity. With this kind of temporary assistance, it may be possible to go on and work on the other contributory factors to panic disorder. This is of great benefit for the individual who has yet to go on and develop the necessary skills to deal with anxiety and the stressful events that life regularly presents.

In addition, those whose panic disorder is accompanied by a depression may be further helped by the prescription of a medication that increases the level of a neurotransmitter serotonin. Fluoxetine (Prozac) and clorimipramine (Anafranil) may be helpful in these cases.

The medication should be prescribed by a professional experienced with anxiety-related problems. Sometimes a general practitioner will prescribe a tranquilizer for an anxious patient without further evaluation by a mental health professional. This usually does nothing for the problem except prolong it.

Some of these medications take a considerable length of time, perhaps a month to six weeks, before effects begin. You need to know this before thinking that the prescribed medication is not helpful.

All medications have potential side effects. Be certain you know what these could be. Do not discontinue medications on your own. Many can produce undesirable and even dangerous effects if stopped abruptly. So, when you feel that you may be able to lower the dosage or discontinue the medication altogether, it is wise to discuss it with the physician who prescribed the medication and is monitoring its use. Furthermore, with lengthy use and some dosages, withdrawal symptoms can occur which can add to the anxiety they are being used to treat.

RELAPSE RATES FOR THOSE INDIVIDUALS USING ONLY MEDICATION TO CONTROL ANXIETY, PHOBIA AND PANIC ARE VERY HIGH.

Medication has a definite role in the treatment of anxiety. These drugs are beneficial in controlling symptoms in the short-term--while you gain skills in changing the way you eat, think and act, and while you discover self-help methods which will allow you to control and overcome anxiety-related problems.

MEDICATION CAN TEMPORARILY HELP TO LIMIT THE SYMPTOMS--USE THEM FOR A WHILE IF YOU MUST--BUT THE REAL ANSWER IS IN NATURAL MEANS WHICH YOU CONTROL YOURSELF.

Gerri's Dog Dilemma

Gerri was absolutely terrified of dogs, any kind of dogs. She thought she remembered being chased by a barking, snarling dog as a child but she didn't remember the details. She always avoided dogs, never wanted to own one or pet one. But, if she visited a home where there was one and it appeared to be well-behaved, she was OK with it being in the room.

Shortly after her divorce, Gerri had her first phobic attack. She was standing on the curb when she felt something wet behind her leg. Turning, she realized that a blind person with a seeing-eye dog was waiting to cross behind her, and what she had felt was the dog's nose. When the light changed and they all began to cross the street, Gerri's heart started to pound. Her legs were so weak she couldn't pull herself up onto the opposite curb. The seeing-eye dog and its master passed her by and that was, according to Gerri's thinking, the beginning of her real dog phobia.

After that, Gerri couldn't pass a house where a dog was living, even if the dog was only sleeping on the front porch and ignoring her completely. She began to think about dogs all the time. She suddenly became aware just how many dog calendars and little dog figurines and dog books there were. Everywhere Gerri looked, there was something about dogs. Gerri was becoming obsessed with the thought of avoiding thinking about dogs.

When Gerri went to her doctor to "do" something about her dog phobia, he thought it was quite humorous. "Well, now Gerri, dogs are man's best friend, don't you know that?" he laughed.

However, he was persuaded to give her a prescription for a tranquilizer. "Maybe you'll calm down with this," he said. His parting shot was the best indication that he had no concept of how serious phobias and panic can be. He joked, "That should take the bite out of your fear of dogs." Gerri felt her face flush and her anger rise to the surface immediately, but she only thanked him and took the prescription. It was all too apparent he thought Gerri was being foolish. She left his office feeling stupid and angry and she vowed to never go to this doctor again.

By this time Gerri was willing to try anything and she found, with the tranquilizer, that she felt a lot more comfortable. It was so easy! She couldn't believe that she had allowed herself to suffer so long. Just take her medication and she was fine. She was even able to pass dogs being walked on leashes when she met them on the street. She told herself that she had it conquered.

Gerri made the same mistake millions make. After a while, either the medication requires a higher dosage to be effective, or decreasing the dosage, or stopping the medication completely, results in withdrawal symptoms that are extremely uncomfortable.

Gerri did exactly that. She began to feel she was over her fear, she didn't ever want to talk to that doctor again, and she hated remembering to take her pills. She decided one day to discontinue her medication on her own. Within 8 hours Gerri suffered withdrawal symptoms she had not anticipated. She was shaking and sweating and felt she could feel every sound "beating against her skin." Her withdrawal symptoms were so uncomfortable and so obvious, she couldn't go to work. She had to call in sick.

Worse yet, she found that she had actually made no progress in her dog phobia. Her phobia was back big-time, and the dread of it was even worse than before. In addition, Gerri was filled with self-recrimination that she had wasted all this time doing, as she put it "nothing about the damn dogs."

Gerri had learned the hard way that medication alone is not the answer to anxiety, panic or phobia. It is only a stop-gap measure to decrease or make the symptoms tolerable while other things which are at the root of the disorder are addressed.

Gerri had a number of the high-anxiety personality traits and most of the time she considered them beneficial. She was a hard worker, punctual and precise. When she realized that her "dog-crazies," as she termed it, were back, she also realized it was time to get some professional help.

Now divorced and self-supporting, living alone and lying awake night after night, the worrying about the "what if" had to stop. WHAT IF she should have to pass a dog to get to work? WHAT IF a dog caused her to be late? Or, worst of all, WHAT IF being unable to confront a dog caused her to be unable to get to work at all? Gerri had to do something to make her life tolerable.

In addition, because she lived alone, Gerri opted for microwave living, sometimes just popping a frozen dinner in or having a bowl of cereal. In the morning she would only have black coffee, because she needed more time to work around any dogs she might have to pass on her way. Sometimes she would have a snack out of the machine mid-morning, sometimes nothing at all until lunch.

Phobias, Panic and Fear--Oh, My!

Scientists funded by NIMH are investigating the basic thought processes and emotions that come into play during phobias and panic attacks, and those that contribute to the development and persistence of agoraphobia. The Institute supports research which evaluates the impact of various versions of cognitive-behavioral therapy and the effects of interpersonal stress such as marital conflict on the disorder. In studying the thought processes and emotions of sufferers of these disorders, NIMH is evaluating the differing anxiety disorders on the basis of what it is that the individual fears.

The anxiety disorders all differ in what the individual fears, how persistent the fear is and how high the level of anxiety becomes. Knowing just what this is can provide a clue to the exact disorder for a correct diagnosis and ultimately, the proper treatment.

Adjustment Disorders

Everyday activities provide a level of anxiety that did not exist before. If this high level of anxiety occurs within three months after a stressful event and does not last longer than six months, then it is classified as an adjustment disorder.

Post-traumatic Stress Disorder

The threatening event is of such magnitude (such as murder, war, natural disaster) that it is outside the range of normal human experience.

Simple Phobia

The fear is of something that is not normally dangerous or frightening, sufficient for the individual to avoid the subject.

Social Phobia

The fear is caused by the scrutiny of others.

Obsessive-Compulsive Disorder

The fear is of losing control. Ritual behavior is instituted in an effort to avoid that loss.

Uncomplicated Panic Disorder

Panic attacks occur without the association of a specific threat.

Panic with Agoraphobia

Fear of the possibility of being powerless while in vulnerable situations.

Generalized Anxiety Disorder

Two or more subjects that should not be anxiety-provoking provoke persistent and chronic levels of anxiety.

They're BAAAACK!

"Working with the therapist I became 'desensitized' over a period of weeks and months. I doubt that I will ever own a dog, but I can handle being around one now and that is all I want to do," reported Gerri.

The professional Gerri found was a behavioral therapist and together they began a program specifically for phobias.

Behaviorists believe that these disorders originate in the individual's tendency to underestimate his or her problem-solving abilities while overestimating the threat in a situation. Originally the person associates a neutral object or action with another negative stimulus. Without knowing exactly what had happened, the therapist believed something negative occurred in Gerri's childhood that became associated with dogs.

By avoiding dogs, Gerri avoided that anxiety, whatever its negative stimulus had originally been.

The behaviorist began by teaching Gerri some relaxation techniques to help her remain calm.

The behaviorist then used a technique known as systematic desensitization. Gerri drew up a list of her fears (for example, from seeing a dog photo to having a huge, snarling, barking dog jump at her throat). Under the guidance of the therapist, she imagined these things happening, progressing from the least to the most terrifying. Then she worked on mental dialogue. She learned to confront her fear while telling herself that no harm would come to her.

Next came exposure therapy. Accompanied by the therapist she began to take short excursions into the world of dogs. They began by going to pet shops, places where the animals were caged. Then a well-trained obedient dog, held on a leash by a professional dog handler, was brought into the treatment and Gerri was able to pet the dog, although reluctantly. All the time Gerri worked on relaxation techniques and mental dialogue.

Eventually Gerri's attacks lessened and she was able to begin to put dogs in their proper perspective in her life.

A year went by. "Out of the blue," Gerri had a panic attack. She was hesitant to phone the therapist because she felt she had somehow let her down. She asked herself, "Why am I doing this to myself?" But Gerri finally did call and she found out it is not unusual to have relapses, that panic attacks and phobias are intertwined.

Gerri had had medication and behavioral therapy. NOW WHAT?

"The first time in treatment, I was looking for the therapist to solve my problems. I readily entered into the desensitization program but when she talked to me about diet and sleep and things like that, I dismissed it as being unimportant." Gerri now realized that whatever treatment she chose next, she HAD to learn to change her thinking as well as some of her ways of living.

Gerri began to do a lot of reading and soon found that a lot of the work she had to do involved changing herself. It wasn't easy but she gave up caffeine. One of the most difficult parts was changing her diet. "I guess I lived on sugar," laughed Gerri. "Living alone I had gotten used to never really shopping for groceries or cooking anything very complicated. It was all frozen dinners, yogurt, an apple, a candy bar or a doughnut, and lots of coffee. Once I was convinced how important diet was, I discovered that I really enjoy cooking! Now I prepare lots of stews and soups with vegetables which I can prepare ahead and have for several days--and I'm saving money too." Gerri is working with a therapist again, this time working on cognitive aspects of her problem PLUS changing her own behavior. "This time I am going to really work on it and not expect a therapist to cure me," said Gerri.

Chapter 8
Various Treatments

THERE ARE MANY TREATMENTS AVAILABLE, but most of them fall into three broad-based groups: psychodynamic, humanistic-existentialist and behavioral.

Psychodynamic Psychotherapy

Freudian psychiatrists are in disagreement with others who follow the modified and expanded teachings of Jung, Adler and Erikson. Such psychotherapy can be beneficial for those who suffer from long-range mental difficulties in conjunction with the anxiety, phobic and panic disorders. This type of treatment can take a number of years to complete.

While this approach views the cause coming not just from external forces but from the internal struggle between the unconscious mind and the conscious mind, it completely ignores the physical causes involved in anxiety disorders.

Humanistic-Existential Therapy

This therapy sees the conflict between the person's view of a desired personality and the reality of self.

The anxiety is caused by conflict between a negative self-concept and the inability to attain the ideal self.

The goal of such therapy is to create an emotional environment in which change can occur. This too, ignores the physical involvement in anxiety disorders.

Behaviorial-Cognitive Therapy

Most behaviorists acknowledge that thought, emotion, expectation and interpretation of observable behavior and the external forces color our response to our environment. They often believe that the anxiety disorders come from an individual's tendency to underestimate his or her ability to solve problems while overestimating the threat.

These therapists use treatments such as desensitization, neuro-linguistic program removal, paradoxical intention, and medication.

Several variations in a cognitive-behavior approach to treatment have shown significant efficacy in the reduction and/or elimination of anxiety disorders, including panic attacks. Published reports from several research centers indicate that a vast majority of patients are panic free at the end of a course of cognitive-behavioral treatment.

Since the personality aspect of panic disorder may be the most difficult for you to view objectively, sessions with such a therapist may be beneficial.

Behavioral-cognitive therapy requires work on the part of the patient. It is not possible to sit back and let the therapist do it all. These sessions usually begin with the individual making a list of the situations she usually avoids.

The therapist and the patient then discuss the symptoms that develop when these phobic situations occur. By talking rationally about the physical symptoms in a safe setting and examining just how they trigger further symptoms, they can be used to "signal" coping strategies when an actual panic attack occurs. However, this takes work and practice in this safe environment. The therapist leads the patient through practice in breathing, relaxation techniques and thought control. The patient will need to make a list of goals to be achieved, such as moving from the least fearful--looking at a photograph of the frightening situation to actually being in the situation--without panic.

After relaxation techniques and symptoms signaling are thoroughly practiced, the difficult work of cognitive strategy begins. Negative and self-defeating thoughts are identified and constructive thoughts are substituted. "I can't stand another minute of this" or "This is terrible, I really am going to die" must be replaced with positive thoughts such as, "I know this will pass in a few minutes as long as I do not allow it to run away with my thoughts," that will become automatic when the signaling physical symptoms begin. During these sessions the therapist works with the patient to identify the personality traits and automatic thinking processes that need to be altered or decreased in order to implement the control of panic attacks.

The "Why" of Self-Defeating Thinking

Susan's life was being destroyed by panic attacks. She often had them at work and went to great lengths to disguise the fact because she thought everyone would either laugh at her or think she was crazy. In the process of working with the behavioral-cognitive therapist, she had readily learned the symptom signaling and relaxation techniques, but when it came to understanding herself and her thinking, she was totally unable to see herself objectively.

Susan grew up in an alcoholic household. Her father, who was, in her words, "a great guy and very funny--when he was sober," had led her and her mother into a world of anguish and fear.

"When my father was drinking he was

another person entirely," said Susan. "I realize now that we never knew what he would be like until he walked in that front door in the evening. If he stayed out drinking and my mother and I went to bed, he would turn on all the lights and curse and yell that we didn't care if he was alive or dead. If we waited up for him, he would curse and yell that we were checking up on him, waiting to see if he was drunk and what time he came home. I dreaded the sound of his key in the door and I would be flooded with relief if he was coming in sober.

"I know it is difficult to understand, but until I talked this over with the therapist I didn't realize that not only was I overly fearful of authority figures but I was also trapped by rigid thinking. I began to trace my panic attacks to problems at work when I would have to talk to my boss. I believed that every time he spoke to me it was going to be to tell me I had done something wrong. My heart would start to thump and I would begin to get shaky.

"After we examined it over a period of a few weeks, weeks when I kept a journal, I saw that the boss had spoken to me over fifty times, and none of those conversations were in any way bad, I just had expected them to be.

"It is the most difficult part of the whole process, changing my way of viewing people in authority--policemen, the lady at the library when I return overdue books, even things in the mail that have an unfamiliar but official-looking return address--I am very slowly learning that all of these people are not going to be angry with me."

Desensitization

Desensitization is the technique of repeating and increasing exposure to the situation or object that triggers anxiety. In controlled stages, the therapist leads the patient up to and through the experience-- again and again--practicing coping strategies and building up tolerance.

Neuro-linguistic Programming Removal

Neuro-linguistic programming removal is another technique. Working with a therapist, you are asked to relax and imagine you are in a theatre, watching a screen. You are led as you imagine good thoughts and feelings about yourself. The therapist leads you through a series of "in control" experiences. One arm becomes the anchor and the therapist touches it lightly to "anchor" positive thoughts there. Then you are asked to see yourself on the movie screen in a situation that arouses your phobia. The feeling is then "anchored" to your other arm by the therapist. Good and bad feelings are anchored, one on top of the other, on each arm. The therapist then proceeds to help you to lose the bad anchors and retain the good ones. Ultimately, you should be able to deal with the phobias as the skilled technique of the therapist has assisted you to integrate these feelings until all the negative ones have gone.

Paradoxical Intention Therapy

Paradoxical intention therapy also requires the assistance of a therapist. For example, if you become so fearful that you might faint, your therapist would say, "Do it. Faint!" After several attempts, you discover that you are unable to faint, and your anxiety diminishes. The therapist continues to repeat such a procedure in selected settings until you experience little or no anxiety. The therapist leads you through doing the opposite of what you might be naturally inclined to do during an attack. Deliberately intensifying the symptoms eventually reduces the anxiety and weakens the attack.

Although paradoxical intention therapy may eliminate panic symptoms in some cases, it does not focus on underlying issues that contribute to the attacks. Dr. David H. Barlow, director for the Center for Stress and Anxiety Disorders at the State University of New York at Albany, is a proponent of behavior therapy to desensitize patients to panic through a process he calls reality testing. He explains: "Although panic disorder sufferers know rationally that what they fear isn't going to happen, they attribute their avoidance of horrible consequences to some outside force, such as luck or timing."

That reliance on outside forces keeps them chained to their illness. Barlow teaches patients that their symptoms need not signal danger. Because the reality testing is gradual, its effects are lasting, he says: "People feel they've really learned something."

Self-Help

What most sufferers want most is to end the panic. You want to stop the disorder and to be in control of your life.

There are a number of things that you can do, and you can begin now. Diet, exercise, visualization and fantasy, meditation and thought stopping are all techniques you can learn--without a therapist, without expensive medications, without having to do anything but MAKE CHANGES in how you live your life. Once you make these changes you will see an incredible difference in how you feel, think and act. Only you can make these changes.

THE FUTURE IS WHERE YOU ARE GOING TO SPEND THE REST OF YOUR LIFE.

While many of these techniques are recommended by psychologists, doctors, even dentists for patients who feel overly anxious, you must implement them. Learning them is easy, but expect to practice them every day.

The best approach to anxiety disorders is prevention. CHANGE YOUR DIET, EXERCISE, GIVE UP CAFFEINE--you can do all of these things. Whether you learn relaxation techniques or simply learn to think more positively, you need to find a way to be a well-rounded, whole person who nurtures each part of yourself. If you don't service your car, it breaks down, and if you don't take care of yourself, you break down.

Support Groups

It is most important for sufferers to realize they are not alone, and many experts encourage joining a support group.

Chapter 9
Treatment for Simple Phobia

THROUGH GRADUAL, SUPERVISED EXPOSURE, you can relearn activities you have been avoiding. Ideally, a family member or friend should be enlisted as a guide, both for emotional support and for encouragement.

The procedure is straightforward: You enter the feared situation and stay as long as possible. The person who has become phobic about using elevators should stand near the elevator bank, for example, watching the riders come and go. When you no longer experience symptoms in that situation, you are ready to stand in the elevator with the doors held open. When you can do that for several minutes without experiencing symptoms, try a one or two floor ride. If the exposure level becomes too difficult, the guide or therapist allows you to backslide one level. In this case, allowing you to stand in the open elevator until the symptoms remit. It is important that both you and your guide have concrete goals, say an hour of watching people near the elevator bank, an hour to practice standing in the open elevator, etc.

The duration of real-life exposure to the phobic stimulus is critical; the object is to pair relaxation with the phobic experience. You should have direct contact, that is a ride in the elevator, during the first session. The patient and the guide or therapist should repeat the exercise frequently, and sessions should be 1 1/2 to 3 hours long. Short sessions may worsen the phobia.

One difficulty that often becomes apparent during treatment is that a panic patient may have lost perspective of a normal anxiety level. You may be likely to view any feelings of anxiety as potentially catastrophic. For this reason, it is helpful if the guide is either a professional therapist or someone who has a thorough understanding of the problem and the patience to follow through on the time it takes to experience the therapy.

You should seek a therapist who is comfortable discussing various theories about panic and anxiety and beware of anyone who claims his or hers is the only valid treatment.

A Safe Place

All panic disorder and phobia sufferers should construct a mental safe place for themselves. This is done at a time when you are relaxed and safely at home, or wherever it is that you are not likely to be controlled by your fear.

After relaxing, visualize in great detail a place where you can be totally safe. It can be anywhere: a room within a vault that only you know the combination to open; a castle surrounded by a moat; an island populated with robots that are totally at your command. It really doesn't matter where it is but you should furnish it completely, in as much detail as you can think of and KNOW that you are safe in this place. Practice visualizing it regularly. Go there to rest or sleep or read. Go there to be safe and secure while you recharge your batteries.

If you wish, you can have an "angel" who protects you there, who listens to your fears and dreams, who hears you talk about your day and comforts you. This is your very own protector--it could be a person or an animal--that is unimportant. What is important is that you create this protector and he/she has only one job: to listen to you.

If you feel anxiety beginning, go to your safe place, slow down your breathing and relax your muscles. You may be able to prevent an attack. Once you have done this once, you will know that it is possible to do it again.

Imagery Desensitization

Visualization and calming self-talk can help to eliminate phobias. List your fears from the most fearful to the least. Start with the least fearful thing.

Desensitization involves disconnecting the association of fright from the phobic situation or object.

You begin by desensitizing the phobic object in your mind only. With relaxation techniques and imagery, go to that mental safe place where you are completely in control. Be conscious of your breathing, making it slow and even, from your diaphragm. Then bring in the feared object or experience. For example, if you fear crossing bridges, sit on a hilltop by your castle or your island and only observe the bridge from a very safe distance.

Use your creativity and imagine the bridge in different colors, sizes or shapes. Imagine different backgrounds. Picture yourself smiling and being strong as you approach the bridge. Create the visualization of yourself walking firmly across the bridge and when you get to the other side, smile and shake your fist at the bridge in triumph.

Daily visualization for twenty minutes at a time is helpful. It may take several weeks before you notice any effect but imagery desensitization can reduce anxiety sufficiently to make the task of real-life desensitization possible.

Chapter 10
Treatment of Panic Disorder

BEHAVIORAL THERAPY, aimed at helping you confront fearful situations and develop coping skills, and cognitive therapy, aimed at treating panic attacks directly by restructuring self-defeating thought processes, may be beneficial.

Some experts feel that psychotherapy alone will not combat panic disorder. However, some feel that it is of value in helping patients get back on the subway, into their cars or offices to function despite the anxiety this may create.

Since many victims are convinced of their own complicity and the need for secrecy, since they feel extremely embarrassed by the disorder, therapy may require some time before it is possible to break through this thinking.

When Should Cognitive Behavioral Therapy End?

The National Institute of Health recommends that any treatment that fails to produce an effect within eight weeks should be reassessed.

In most cases, panic disorder is chronic and it waxes and wanes in severity. For some, it is only a short-term problem that never recurs, while others may suffer a severe chronic illness. Individuals with agoraphobia tend to have a more severe and complicated illness.

Since much remains to be learned about the long-term effectiveness of maintenance doses of medication, psychotherapy and life-style changes, it is best, according to Thomas Unde of the National Institute of Mental Health, to use medication to allay symptoms for six to 12 months, while you work on other aspects of the disorder.

Anxiety and Depression

It is understandable that many patients suffering from anxiety disorders are depressed. Living with excessive anxiety, phobias that disrupt life, and the exhaustion that comes with panic attacks could make even the strongest individual depressed.

Anxiety disorder patients are often ashamed of their illness and find depression a more acceptable diagnosis and explanation for their problems.

Researchers have noted the connection between anxiety and depression. Recent studies have supported this connection. One such study found that 50 percent of patients diagnosed as depressed first came for treatment with panic attack symptoms. Another study reported that the presence of major depression produced a tremendous increased risk for panic disorder.

For individuals who are diagnosed as suffering from both depression and anxiety disorder, treatment of the underlying depression may be necessary before treatment of the panic disorder can begin.

Chapter 11
The Self-Help Answer

Generalized Anxiety Disorder

Generalized anxiety is often a "catch-all" term for people who live rather stressed lives. The job, the mortgage, the kids, the commute, the hours, the bills--who hasn't felt that they were so stressed that they could just pull their hair out?

Going home, sitting down in front of the TV with a couple of beers is not the answer to this kind of anxiety and stress.

Exercise--30 minutes daily.

Remove--alcohol, caffeine and limit sugar. In some instances, this is sufficient to eliminate the symptoms.

Behavioral therapy may be beneficial.

Relaxation and meditation techniques.

Social Phobia

Social phobia is the fear of embarrassment or humiliation that could occur when engaging in an activity in front of others.

Social phobia closely resembles performance anxiety or "stage fright," and has many national health consequences. Many individuals who suffer from social phobia turn to alcohol and/or illegal drugs for temporary relief and social phobia is considered a cause of alcoholism and drug abuse.

Exercise--a vigorous exercise regime will greatly benefit the tension of the social phobic.

Remove--alcohol and caffeine.

Relaxation techniques to relieve muscle tension.

Rehearsal of performance in a non-threatening environment and good preparation of speeches or talks to aid self-confidence that the material and the speaker are well prepared.

PMS and the Panic Disorder Connection

Mood swings are the most common symptom of PMS. Tension, depression, fatigue, irritability, sleep disturbance, backache, migraine, sinus congestion, weight gain, asthma, epilepsy, loss of sense of smell, dizziness, acne, food cravings and panic disorder are some of the more than one hundred fifty symptoms of PMS.

PMS is not the same as painful menstruation, which is often treatable with estrogen. Nor is it the same as menstrual distress, a condition marked by symptoms that persist throughout a woman's cycle, worsening just prior to the onset of menstruation.

Recent research suggests that PMS is a progesterone response disorder. The problem is not a deficiency of the female sex hormone progesterone. Rather, it is an inhibition of the body's progesterone receptors, which do not allow the hormone to function where it is needed. Often physicians will test a women for progesterone levels in her blood and find they are within normal limits. The difficulty does not lie in the production of the hormone, but in the receptors for the uptake of the hormone, such as those in the brain's limbic system.

Progesterone receptors are found in the uterus, as well as many other parts of the body. The largest concentration lies in the brain's limbic area. Impaired uptake of progesterone in this area may account for the emotional symptoms of PMS, including tension, violent outbursts and panic disorder.

Progesterone receptors in the nasal passages, lungs, eyes, breasts and liver may explain other common PMS symptoms, including sinus pain, hoarseness, glaucoma and breast soreness.

Another key function of progesterone is to help regulate levels of the sugar glucose in the bloodstream. Glucose levels that fall too low can trigger irritability, headache, fainting, crying and panic attacks. And as stored sugar is taken from cells, the cells fill up with water. The result: water retention and weight gain.

Two out of three women who attended the first PMS clinic in the world at University College Hospital, London, England and were treated by Dr. Katharina Dalton, responded to a simple change in diet. THESE WOMEN REQUIRED NO OTHER TREATMENT. The diet:

Every three hours, eat a small amount of a starchy food--bread, crackers, cereal, potatoes, corn, rice. Do not increase the number of calories you ingest, simply increase the frequency. For example, save a piece of toast from your breakfast and eat it mid-morning instead of some sugary snack. If you have a sandwich for lunch, save one half of it to eat mid-afternoon. By the end of the day you will not have increased your calories, you will only have divided them evenly throughout the day. Do the same with dinner, allowing a small amount of a starchy food to be your bedtime snack so that you will be better able to stabilize your blood sugar through out the night.

The diet must be followed every day, not just prior to menstruation. If too much time passes between snacks or meals, you may start to feel bad again, and that may continue for several days.

This diet works because when you eat a meal,

your glucose level rises, then gradually falls over the next several hours. If no food is eaten after a lengthy interval, the body releases adrenaline to mobilize some of its stored sugar.

Progesterone receptors do not work in the presence of adrenaline--and adrenaline triggers some of the most unpleasant PMS symptoms--including panic, anger and migraine.

The key to controlling PMS--and with it the panic attacks--is to keep the blood sugar level steady. Eating sugar creates a rapid rise and fall in the blood sugar level. It is best, if you must eat sugar, to eat it with a starchy food, not alone.

Caffeine can cause irritability, sleeplessness, jumpiness and headaches at any time, not just during the days leading up to menstruation. Women who wish to end PMS should avoid all sources of caffeine, including coffee, tea and soft drinks.

In addition, women with severe PMS also respond well to progesterone treatment. It is usually taken daily from the start of ovulation until the onset of menstruation. The correct dosage, however, depends on a woman's particular cycle and the rate at which her body absorbs progesterone.

Progesterone is given via suppository or injection--not as a pill. When taken orally, progesterone is absorbed mostly by the liver and never reaches the cells where it is needed.

Although some doctors recommend tubal ligation for women with severe PMS, this minor surgery can actually make PMS symptoms worse. Many doctors also prescribe birth control pills because they are confusing progesteron contained in the pills with progesterone. While birth control pills relieve pain, regularize menstruation and reduce blood flow, they may actually make PMS worse. Hysterectomy also may worsen the symptoms of PMS for six to 12 months following this surgery.

Obsessive-Compulsive Disorder

Obsessive-compulsive disorder is a disease of repetitive thoughts and rituals. Brain-imaging techniques such as computerized tomography, magnetic resonance imaging and photon emission computerized tomography have revealed that these individuals have differences in the brain areas that are associated with movement control, learned behavior and methods of dealing with repetitive stimulations. It is hoped that future research will reveal just how specific neurotransmitter receptor sites perform differently in these individuals. It has been found that individuals with this disorder metabolize glucose at abnormally high rates.

It is recommended that the diet as listed under the section on PMS be undertaken and that treatment with Anafranil (clorimipramine), an antidepressant which appears to be successful in significantly reducing the obsessions and compulsions, be prescribed.

Post-Traumatic Stress Disorder

Improved diet, removal of nicotine, caffeine and junk food sugars should be undertaken.

In addition, since the abuse of alcohol in order to mask feelings may be a problem, membership in AA or some other type of alcohol treatment may be appropriate.

This is one condition where psychotherapy may very well be quite appropriate. Individuals with this disorder often suffer from guilt and shame and need someplace safe where they can "talk it out."

Support groups, such as may be found through the Police Officers' Associations, veteran groups, particularly those with Vietnam veterans, are excellent sources for help.

Chapter 12
Solutions--
Help Yourself Gain Control

Stop Any Attack

When you feel the fear coming on, tell yourself, "These are normal bodily reactions to stress. I just have an exaggerated reaction at the moment."

Let the feelings come. They do not mean that you are sick or that you are going to die. You know that is not true. Don't run away from your panic. As you feel it increase, take a deep abdominal breath and as you let it out, try to let the emotions go out with it. Accept these feelings. You can do it and come through it.

If you are on a street, lean against a building or a pole. If you are in a shop, tell the people there you don't feel well and want to sit down for a few minutes; they will help you. If you are at your desk at work, get up and walk--not run--outside. If you have a thought-stopping rubber band on your wrist--snap it. Don't allow all the what-ifs to run away with your emotions. Accept what is happening to you, look at it. If you do this, the thing that you fear the most WILL NOT HAPPEN.

Think about what is happening within your body. Marvel at the ability of your body to respond to your emotions. It is a wonderful machine that is responding to your commands. Repeat to yourself, "I will not faint. I will not die. I will not lose control" and it will respond to those commands too. Believe this to be true and see that you are right.

Wait a few moments and the fear and the sensations will pass. They have before. You are in the process of conquering panic disorder. You will win. Observe yourself--notice that as you stop adding panicky thoughts to your present attack, the fear starts to dissolve.

Think about the progress you have already made. Distract yourself from what is going on inside you now. Observe your surroundings, see what others are doing but don't interpret their behavior, just observe others going about their business.

As the panic subsides, let your muscles relax. Take a deep breath and shake yourself slightly to increase the loosening of your muscles. You have lived through the panic attack. Each time you are able to do this you are reducing your fear.

After you control a panic attack by yourself, give yourself a pat on the back. You have been brave and not a little courageous.

Now: Take Charge

First, get a complete medical checkup to eliminate any possibility of another medical cause for your symptoms. If there is an additional medical cause, have that treated before you go any further--you may solve your problem right there.

Second, get a proper diagnosis. When you have your medical work-up, INSIST on a five or six-hour blood glucose tolerance test. Out of kilter blood sugars have been greatly implicated in panic disorder and may point the way to dietary therapy.

If the diagnosis is that you have anxiety, panic attacks or phobias, accept that fact. Once armed with a correct diagnosis, you can begin to take charge of your life.

For Those With Anxiety, Panic Attacks and Phobias:

Now that you understand how your biochemistry and the development of personality traits within your family came together--you should know that:

You are not responsible for your biochemistry--but you are responsible to make changes in the kinds of stress you subject it to.

You are not responsible for the kind of family you grew up in--but you are responsible to realistically view the personality traits and perceptual styles you have developed as a result of that upbringing.

You are not responsible for suffering from a phobia or a panic attack. This is a real physical condition with real symptoms. You are neither crazy nor losing your mind.

THINKING IS PRACTICING BODY CHEMISTRY. YOU CREATE CHEMICAL REACTIONS BY WHAT YOU THINK ABOUT WHAT IS HAPPENING IN YOUR LIFE.

So, what is the next step?

1. Recognize you have a physical condition that manifests itself with real physical symptoms.

2. Recognize that this condition is aggravated by stress, and

There are two different kinds of stress:

1. Physical

2. Emotional

YOU CANNOT CHANGE THE PAST. THE FUTURE IS WHERE YOU WILL SPEND THE REST OF YOUR LIFE.

The person who has a small abnormality in brain biochemistry (and this may include you) needs to either increase the block to the stress-inducing chemicals or decrease the chemicals that produce stress/anxiety physical reactions; it may be that you are ingesting them (i.e. caffeine) or you may be producing them by your reaction to external events.

Work on the aspects of your personality that contribute to stress reactions which then lead to anxiety, phobia and panic.

Practicing Body Chemistry

Eliminate Caffeine

The most common saboteur of stamina is caffeine. "People who drink too much coffee may experience palpitations, jitters, and gastrointestinal distress," says Dr. Moreines. "Anyone under stress should avoid caffeine. In fact, caffeine is routinely used to induce panic attacks in clinical experiments. When given doses equivalent to the caffeine in four or five cups of coffee, nearly half of panic disorder patients experienced a reaction that was indistinguishable from a spontaneous panic attack."

This stimulant is sufficient to affect the way your brain and body respond and function. Many people can't start a day without their "wake-up" coffee because they recognize their brain responds to the stimulation caffeine provides. It stimulates the electrical signals to your muscles which, for the phobic individual, can result in excessive responsiveness. For some, even one cup of this stimulant is too much. Caffeine is not only in coffee. Cocoa, chocolate tea, cola drinks, and over-the-counter stimulants such as Up-time and No-Doz all contain caffeine.

At first, without this stimulant, you might have a headache. This is because of the effect on the blood vessels, causing them to contract and limit the blood flow to the brain, which the caffeine user has become accustomed to experiencing. Without the effect of caffeine, the blood vessels expand, causing more blood to flow to the brain, causing that feeling of a "pounding" headache often described by those who attempt to discontinue caffeine. In that case, try reducing your caffeine by a fourth, or a half--until you have eliminated it entirely.

You might want to replace your caffeine with a herb tea. Just sit down and have a cup of relaxing tea--chamomile, as long as you are not allergic to flowers, is beneficial. Peppermint or raspberry teas are some others you might enjoy. They can aid you to relax and re-charge. Herb teas are non-caffeinated and, in addition, have relaxing properties of their own. For example, mint is an antispasmodic which soothes the smooth muscle lining of the digestive tract. (Which explains the popularity of after dinner mints.) Chamomile and raspberry also relax the digestive tract and are pleasantly soothing to the mouth. Don't take a coffee break--take a herbal tea break instead.

Eliminate Nicotine

Nicotine, the stimulating ingredient in cigarettes,

is absorbed through the mucous lining of the mouth and the lungs, where it is passed into the bloodstream and is circulated to the brain. Nicotine triggers a variety of responses in the nervous system. It acts on the hypothalamus, the control center of a number of vital functions, and can affect the cardiovascular system, causing rapid heartbeat. It increases cardiac output, constricts the blood vessels and elevates blood pressure.

Eliminate Alcohol

Alcohol has effects on all body systems and it can create feelings of anxiety, insomnia and tremor. While it may seem to be relaxing at the time, the process of metabolizing it requires, and then finally uses up, all the body's B vitamins, as well as having many other negative effects. Rebound symptoms of withdrawal include hyper-alertness with jerky movements and the tendency to be easily startled.

Eliminate Illegal Drugs

Both cocaine and amphetamines are stimulants that interfere with the chemical functioning in the brain. Over time, these drugs replace the natural brain chemicals which normally regulate both mood and perception. After prolonged use, the brain may cease to produce the neurotransmitters that interfere with irritability and other elevated responses, resulting in excessive anxiety and its related mental traumas.

Marijuana intoxication can contribute to the feeling of unreality or depersonalization that the panic sufferer experiences. Since loss of control is often at the root of panic or phobic behavior, this unreality can cause many people to experience extreme panic responses.

Understand the Role of Neurotransmitters

Neurotransmitters block the anxiety messages to the brain.

Serotonin

Serotonin is one of the brain's chemical messengers that has been proven to induce sleep, lower blood pressure, decrease the symptoms of premenstrual syndrome and depression, and is tied to both mood and aggression when released by the pineal gland. It may be that people with panic attacks either have a deficiency in serotonin or an excessive requirement for it.

Tryptophan, the amino acid commonly found in milk and other dairy products such as yogurt and cottage cheese, is a precursor of serotonin. Tryptophan, because of an irregularity in its overseas manufacture, is no longer available for purchase separately. Melatonin is a neurotransmitter which is derived from serotonin which in turn is derived from tryptophan. Serotonin is converted into melatonin and then melatonin, in a very simple enzymatic step, is reduced to breakdown products so there is no accumulation in the cells.

However, Melatonin (for Serotonin) can be purchased as a nutritional supplement. It is produced through fermentation in a manner somewhat similar to the way biotin or many of the B vitamins are produced for consumption in capsule form. It does not appear to have side effects when taken orally and in the proper dosage. Melatonin's task is to set and maintain the internal clock. It governs the biorhythms of the body.

Excessive intake of serotonin has been linked to decreased ability to conceive in some women.

It is best to increase your intake of nutrients such as milk, yogurt, and cottage cheese, which contain tryptophan, the natural precursor to serotonin. Dieters often restrict their intake of the very nutrients needed for health and the milk, yogurt and cottage cheese, which contain this very essential precursor of the neurotransmitters, are all available in low-fat or non-fat varieties and should be included abundantly in your diet.

Serotonin is also the brain chemical that controls how much you eat and your body's cravings for protein and carbohydrates. For most normal-weight people, eating foods rich in tryptophan will increase serotonin in the brain to a level at which appetite is satiated. In addition to the genetically linked cause of low levels of this neurotransmitter, it is thought that years of excessive dieting can create a similar deficit.

Melatonin (for Serotonin) is available through most quality health food stores in 2 mg capsules. One capsule may be taken 2 hours before retiring. It will take several weeks to raise serotonin levels enough for the calming and REM-sleep inducing effects to be felt. There are no known adverse side effects for those who stay within normal levels.

A well-known drug which is a serotonin uptake blocker--that is, it reduces the ability of the nerves to absorb serotonin, leaving more serotonin in the brain and thus improving mood--is Prozac. Much has been written about Prozac and its side effects on a small group of people but it would seem that it actually has fewer side effects than other antidepressants. But natural serotonin which is derived from the amino acid tryptophan from dairy product intake in the diet is without side effects. Why take an artificial drug when you can achieve the same effect through proper diet?

Gamma-Aminobutyric Acid (GABA)

GABA is a neurotransmitter that lowers the excitory level of the messages from the limbic system. The body manufacturers its own. Some individuals either do not produce a sufficient amount or their need for this neurotransmitter is greater than others. GABA is an inhibitory neuron which dampens or eliminates its target cells' firing. In addition, GABA also helps to tune-out the specific responsiveness of the excitory networks that convey and interpret information about the external world. GABA is available from your local health food store in combination with B complex vitamins, as they also lower the levels of lactate in the blood.

If you wish to supplement GABA, take one 750-mg dose of GABA three times a day after meals.

If you wish to purchase GABA in its pure form, it is available from the Pain and Stress Center in San Antonio, Texas (1-800-669-2256 or 210-614-7246).

Prior to an event that you know brings on phobic reactions or panic, such as flying, open a capsule and sprinkle 1/2 under your tongue for quick absorption, or dissolve in water.

Dimethylglycine (DMG)

Individuals who are prone to panic attacks often have elevated levels of lactic acid in their bloodstreams, leading many experts to believe that the cause of panic attacks involves the chemistry of the brain or a malfunctioning of overly sensitive chemoceptors. Researchers at the Washington University School of

Medicine have observed that positron emission tomography of patients with panic disorders have an unequal flow of blood through the parahippocampal gyrus, a region of the brain that is thought to mediate anxiety.

Researchers have speculated that the blood-brain barrier may be defective in these patients, allowing substances such as lactate to reach the brain and induce the attack.

Dimethylglycine is a chemical that improves stamina during exercise. It will prevent the buildup of lactic acid, the cause of muscle soreness after exercise and, in some individuals, the triggering of panic attacks. Dimethylglycine will increase oxygen uptake and improve the nutritional environment of the cells.

It is available as either gluconic DMG or dimethylglycine in most better health food stores. If it is not available in your area it can be ordered by mail from Hedendal Chiropractic and Nutrition Center, 301 Crawford Blvd., Boca Raton, Florida 33432 (800-726-8404--voice or 407-391-5279--twenty-four hour fax order line).

Stress Management and Self-Talk

Stressful situations are all around us. If we choose to let them rule our mind and body, we can become tired and overwhelmed or develop stress-related conditions, both physical and mental. The fight-or-flight response, that dramatic reaction that prepares us to fight or run when threatened causes physiological changes which include an elevation in blood pressure, heart rate, respiration, metabolism, epinephrine production, blood glucose, peripheral vascular constriction, pupil dilation and a decrease in testosterone levels.

We actually encounter very few situations in our complex world that force us to actually fight or run, but our bodies still prepare us for action as if we are still cave men, surviving in a hostile life-threatening environment. As a result, muscles and blood vessels constrict, leading to potential problems with breathing, comfort, digestion and elimination. When that stress is chronic, temporary tensing can become permanent tightness, turning transient high blood pressure into persistent hypertension and stomach upset into chronic colitis or ulcers. Stress has been related to many pathological conditions, including headaches, peptic ulcers, arthritis, colitis, diarrhea, asthma, cardiac arrhythmias, sexual problems, circulatory dysfunctions, muscle tension, and cancer.

Change is often characterized as stressful, but not every change is stressful for all people. Stress is not inherent in events themselves. WE DEFINE WHAT

IS UPSETTING FOR US, and our bodies and minds react accordingly. So, each person has to assess the situations that can lead to stress inside and take steps to reduce troublesome reactions.

YOU CANNOT CHANGE THE PAST.

Dwelling on past wrongs or hurts and regrets about the "what ifs" in life will not change them.

THE FUTURE IS WHERE YOU ARE GOING TO SPEND THE REST OF YOUR LIFE.

Stress Awareness

One of the best ways to discover the causes of your stress is to keep a Stress Awareness Diary. This tool will allow you to record when stressful events occur and the subsequent appearance of any emotional or physical symptoms. For example, after a heated disagreement with a colleague, you develop a headache. You may have converted the tension of that situation into tightening muscles in your neck and shoulders, which block circulation and set the stage for the pain of a headache.

Eventually, it is possible to recognize situations that precipitate tension, identify the muscles you tighten in response, and take steps to relax them. Keeping a record of progress will help you change the way your body reacts because it reinforces success and points out what you need to work on in the future.

It is possible to look at personality factors in the initiation of stress and work on them by self-help methods, and you might choose to do that.

If you have chosen to work with a therapist on the areas of personality which cause you to view some situations as threatening and which perhaps constantly contributes to stress, this is a good way to review these areas of personality in a non-threatening situation. You may learn how your past conditioning has helped you view certain situations in a way that is negative, that contributes to your stress, and take steps to change the way you see the world.

Abdominal Breathing

Breathing is a powerful way to energize and relax. Many of us spend a lifetime breathing from the upper part of our chest, never fully aerating our lungs. When stressed, we breathe faster and shallower, making us feel even worse. To counter this reaction, breathe deeply and slowly. Place a hand on your abdomen to make sure you're deep-breathing (the abdomen expands as you breathe in) and inhale to the count of four. Hold that breath for a count of sixteen--the optimum time to fully oxygenate blood and activate the lymphatic system. Then exhale for a count of eight, while imagining the elimination of toxins and the circulation of oxygenated blood to all parts of the body.

You may discover this is difficult to do, particularly if you have been upper-diaphragmatic breathing for a large portion of your life. You haven't experienced this abdominal breathing, so you don't know how to do it. You must practice until it becomes comfortable. You may have to practice regularly to work up to holding your breath for 16 seconds. When you do, complete 10 breaths this way. You will notice a difference in how you feel. Try this in the morning at the sink while washing your face, on the way to a difficult meeting, or after an anxious encounter.

When fatigued, try this deep-breathing technique. While holding your breath, tap on your chest with your fingertips, moving your hand around so that the whole chest is covered. Try tapping your upper back also. Practice these methods regularly to invigorate your daily routine. Tapping stimulates circulation and body awareness. Try to feel the air in the area you are tapping. Try it, it will make you realize how constricted your breathing is. This light tapping is both invigorating and relaxing. But remember, light tapping, only.

Hatha Yoga

Yoga is an ancient method of relaxation, breathing, meditation and mind control. There are entire books written on the subject, particularly the practice of hatha yoga, the yoga of controlling the breath. If you are interested, it is possible to find a number of books on the subject at your local library.

Yoga is a system of controlled breathing which has been practiced for centuries and its structured stretching, slow exercise of the total musculature of the body, and regular breathing might be something you might want to explore to increase your control over your own body and the way you breathe in times of stress.

Meditation

Although people who suffer from panic attacks are often advised to practice relaxation techniques, psychologist David H. Barlow reported that relaxation methods can actually induce panic attacks in some individuals. Some people who undergo panic attacks are acutely sensitive to their bodily sensations and react with panic to the loss of control that appears to occur during relaxation. Barlow and his coworkers at the State University of New York at Albany reported that the supervised relaxation of meditation techniques can help reduce panic attacks after the individuals learn to understand the effects of the loss of control and the sensations experienced.

In a study reported in the *American Journal of Psychiatry* it was found that twenty of twenty-two men and women with anxiety and panic disorders experienced significant reductions in anxiety and depression after undergoing an 8-week meditation course. In this formal meditation practice, the patients were encouraged to develop moment-to-moment awareness, which led to a mindful calmness that undermined anxious feelings and gave them more of a sense of control.

Meditation, which was once thought to just be the province of mystics and yogis has entered the mainstream. Doctors, psychiatrists, and dentists are recommending that patients with anxiety learn to meditate.

There are many different meditation techniques, such as Zen, Buddhist and transcendental meditation (TM is among the most popular). It doesn't matter what kind of meditation you do, they are all useful. The point is to be with yourself and let go of muscle tension and anxiety-provoking thought patterns.

Meditation is like a game of tennis or a dance. The goal is to clear your mind and enjoy what you are doing while you're doing it, not to get to the end. You must train both your mind and body if you want to have self-control and remain calm under pressure. It is a way of focusing attention and altering the level of awareness. It can be structured or unstructured, involving mentally directing feelings and thoughts in a relaxed state through silent conversations or chants, or focusing on an idea or an object. Meditation is traditionally connected to religious practices but that is not necessary for the benefits you might seek in your pursuit of a solution to anxiety attacks.

To learn more about concentration and breathing techniques involved in meditation, you may want to read one of the many books written about meditation. *How to Meditate*, by Lawrence LeShan and *Meditation: A Practical Guide to a Spiritual Discipline*, by Thomas McCormick and Sharon Fish, are both good choices. Another option is to enroll in a course at one of the many transcendental-meditation centers throughout the world. TM has the greatest number of scientific studies to "prove" its usefulness, and it has been found to reduce anxiety and increase energy and self-esteem.

Meditation is not a magic bullet, however. "It isn't recommended for crisis situations," says Kenneth Kline, a clinical psychologist who practices and teaches TM. "If your boyfriend breaks up with you, you're not going to feel like sitting down and meditating. But if you are too anxious to study or you're stressed out at work, I'd recommend you try it. TM helps you reintegrate so you bring more of yourself to the solution."

Klein suggests that anyone having problems with a superior at work, for example, take their coffee break and meditate instead. "It takes the edge off, and afterward you'll feel less angry and more able to deal with the situation. The point is not to get rid of the angry feelings but to use them productively."

Interrupting Negative Images

When you recall the times you felt helpless or victimized it is very easy to replay them over and over in your mind, and to recall them in the identical manner each time you think of them. All that type of thinking does is to reinforce the negative thinking and the negative image of yourself as a helpless person or a victim. When such a thought comes into your mind, shift the images. Make them brighter or dimmer, make the accompanying sounds louder or softer and the speed at which things happen faster or slower. By changing the image in some way that you can control, it loses its power. This is a method to aid you in gaining a sense of control by becoming actively involved in managing your thoughts.

If it is a recent event, such as your boss lecturing you about an error, speed up his voice, make it squeaky, just like a little mouse voice. Change the lighting, the time of day, the clothing, anything that alters the image. When you have done this frequently, you will find that the image becomes either silly or laughable--either way, its power is diminished.

If there is someone who has frightened you, about whom you have unresolved problems left over from previous or childhood struggles, they are often accompanied with feelings of pain and rage. Imagine this person in a jail cell and you have the only key. This is where you can move into the area of positive fantasy.

If unpleasant experiences play over and over in your mind like a bad record, replay them by visualizing them from differing locations. Have the encounters take place in front of you, see them from above, from the side. If you review them from differing aspects, the feelings associated with them may very well diminish, if not vanish all together--as long as you are in control of the situation.

Positive Affirmations and Fantasy

"I'm no good at my job." "No one is going to love me." If you find yourself repeating such doom-and-gloom statements on a regular basis, it is no wonder you are stressed out. Defeatist, negative thinking makes us feel terrible about ourselves, robbing us of vitality and creativity. Instead, take a few minutes out of your day to make positive statements to yourself: "I'm a happy, healthy, productive person" or "My life gets better every day."

If you are facing a particularly stressful situation--meeting your boyfriend's family for the first time, for example--it is often helpful to imagine yourself handling things successfully. "One woman I know imagines she is an actress (name your own choice) when she has some difficult task at hand," says therapist Shirley Swede. "She uses her image of herself as that actress to spur herself on, because she (the chosen actress) is always so cool and in control."

Visualization may also be used to vent anger or frustration. If your supervisor at work is making your life miserable, imagine yourself in situations where you are the boss. One therapist even suggests imagining yourself dumping a bucket of cold water on his or her head. "People who have a sense of humor love this technique," says therapist Janet Damon. "You can also write the person a letter detailing all your grievances and really letting yourself go." However: DON'T MAIL THAT LETTER!

Visualization is more effective in relieving anxiety in conjunction with some sort of relaxation technique. Putting yourself in a calm, restful state of mind before you attempt to visualize your thoughts makes you more receptive to your fantasies, makes them more real and as a result, makes your affirmations more effective in altering negative self-talk.

Nothing is worse for your self-esteem than self-criticism. What do you do when you look in the mirror? If you say, "I look pretty good," you have placed a value on yourself. If you say, "I'm too fat, I'm having a bad hair day. My face is sagging, or look at that big pimple," you have placed a negative value on your self. It is this type of critical thinking that is disastrous to your self-esteem. Take action to raise your self-esteem. Give yourself the positive, nurturing self-talk that you truly deserve. Give yourself what you didn't get as a youngster. By visualizing good things happening to you and saying positive affirmations to yourself, you focus away from fear and panic. With time, they will lose their power over you.

Anita's Garden

Anita is a good example of how well positive self-talk works. She feels a lot better now. "I learned to relax. I practice positive affirmations and fantasy. That sounds funny at first, but with practice it can really help you. When I first took a class in relaxation methods, they would present a visual image that I just couldn't relate to," said Anita. "But I had recently taken up gardening as a way to relax and I realized that I had to visualize in a mental place that had some meaning to me. The most important thing to me was to visualize a place where I felt both safe and in control. I have learned to literally cultivate 'the garden' of my mind. Now when I relax, I take myself out to my garden. I walk between the rows of flowers and vegetables, checking the soil and the new growth. I am on alert for any 'bugs' or 'weeds' (my new terms for negative thoughts).

"I weed out the negative thoughts. I actually see myself digging them up and throwing them on a discard heap, just as if I were actually weeding. Then I plant some positive affirmations in their place, thoughts that have meaning to me about my life and my work. The next time I go back to my garden, I check on my positive affirmations, see how they are growing, if they are healthy and if they have any blooms. Sometimes they surprise me," laughed Anita. "I look around this mental garden and I find some things growing there unexpectedly, good things. That surprise is one of the ways that I know that I'm improving in my thinking."

Anita grew serious, "You need to choose a place that is meaningful to you: the beach, a vacation home, a high mountain top: any place where you feel safe and in control.

Then you have to practice your visualiza-
tions, just like you would practice anything
new that you never knew how to do before.
It works, everyone should try it."

Occasionally reward yourself for sticking to positive
affirmation work. Positive reinforcement promotes
enthusiasm and motivation to continue with any program. A daily pat on the back is a good way to keep
yourself up and motivated. All panic disorder sufferers are good at getting down on themselves when
they don't do it right. Give yourself a lift up and
reward yourself when you do.

Biofeedback

Conventionally trained health care practitioners,
including psychologists, psychiatrists, nurses and physical therapists, have used biofeedback techniques since
the 1960s to control autonomic nervous system functions that were traditionally viewed as unchangeable.

Biofeedback uses sophisticated electronic ma-
chines with monitors and leads to give you a more
precise picture of what is going on inside you. You
can learn to improve your health and wellness by
watching a record of your heartbeat, pulse, or blood
volume track across the screen.

Biofeedback has been used to treat many stress
symptoms, including tension headaches, migraines,

hypertension, insomnia, spastic colon, muscle spasm or pain, epilepsy, anxiety, phobic reactions, asthma, stuttering, and teeth grinding. It is very useful to understand that many of the reactions that we think of as automatic can be controlled through learned monitoring. It is possible to lower heart rates, decrease anxiety and minimize phobic reactions, all by observing them, learning to control them and decreasing how they affect systems we once thought were beyond our own control.

An example that can be easily understood is the mood ring, which changes color with the temperature of the hands of the wearer. A heat sensitive stone is the "jewel" in this type of ring, usually found in novelty stores. When the ring has a dark color, the wearer is supposedly in a dark mood. However, muscle tension throughout the arms control the temperature of the hands by restricting or increasing blood flow to the extremities. Using a mood ring, the wearer can relax the arms, increase blood flow and find that the ring has changed to a lighter color, which supposedly indicates a happier mood. By the use of this simple toy, you can learn to relax arm muscle tension by becoming aware of it through this easy visualization tool. This toy can be an aid in understanding the theory behind biofeedback.

If this interests you, health care practitioners in

your area can assist you in finding a professional biofeedback trainer in your area. Professional organizations will furnish information about this technique. You can contact:

American Association of Biofeedback Clinicians
2424 Dempster
Des Plaines, IL 60016

Biofeedback Certification Institute of America
& Association for Applied Psychophysiology
and Biofeedback
10200 West 44th Avenue, Suite 304
Wheatbridge, CO 80033

Biofeedback Society of D.C.
202-298-0651

Relaxation/Self-Hypnosis

Relaxation skills are like any other skills: they require on-going practice. By the active tightening and releasing of gross muscle groups while noting the differences between sensations of tension and relaxation you will increase your ability to identify even mild tension and reduce it. You can either purchase a relaxation/self-hypnosis tape from any book store or you can purchase specially designed audio tapes to relieve muscle tension and stress. These tapes will guide you through a series of progressive relaxation techniques and guided imagery and they can be purchased from:

The National Headache Foundation in Chicago.
1-800-843-2256.

It is also possible to write your own relaxation script, record it and follow it, listening to your own voice instructing you on how to relax. For best results, you should listen to the tape twice daily, morning and evening.

The following is an example of a tape you can record for yourself:

Sitting comfortably or lying flat on the floor with your eyes closed: Each time you exhale, let your breathing move slowly toward your abdomen . . .focus your attention on your feet. . .let your heels sink into the floor. . .floating . . .relaxing. Let that feeling of relaxation and comfort move up your legs, relaxing more and more with each breath. . .let the relaxation move up through your legs and flow through your hips and lower back. . .relaxing more with each breath. . .let your buttocks and groin sink into the floor. . .so relaxed, so comfortable . . .let your lower back and spine sink into the floor. . .becoming more and more relaxed. . .let all the muscles in your back relax. . .picture them getting longer and wider. . .more and more relaxed. . .let any thoughts you have been carrying around your neck roll down your arms and out your fingertips. . .floating, relaxing, breathing. . .let your shoulders relax. . .let your neck relax. . . getting lighter and more comfortable . . .your head floating easily on your neck. . .let that feeling of comfort and relaxation move up your head. . .your jaw is loose. . .your mouth. . .your nose. . .your eyes and the space behind your eyes and the space behind that. . .let your ears relax. . .your forehead . . .your scalp. . .your hair. . .everything is getting more and more relaxed with each breath. . .release old thoughts and unwanted feelings with each exhalation. . .bring in positive and healing energy with each inhalation . . .more and more relaxed . . .when you are ready, slowly open your eyes, feeling relaxed and refreshed, or drift off to sleep if that is your wish. . .remembering you can return to this state of relaxation anytime you want by saying the word r.e.l.a.x. . . .

And you can add other self-hypnotic messages, such as "I feel totally comfortable and relaxed at work."

You can enhance your relaxation experience by picturing your body relaxing. Use a color, symbol or sound--whatever is soothing to you.

You can use imagery as a calming technique by itself. Picture yourself taking a trip to a relaxing and safe place, somewhere you feel comfortable and restful. Smell the scent of that place, hear its sounds, see its sights, feel the sensations, and taste the tastes. Totally immerse yourself in that relaxing spot for a few minutes, then come back to the here and now, refreshed and recharged.

Through imagery it is possible to control body temperature and heart rate. It is not some esoteric trick that can only be done by aged yogis in some far off land. The mind is completely capable of expanding and contracting blood vessels and with it comes the ability to raise and lower your own heart rate.

Picturing a pleasant day ahead and visualizing yourself as confident and relaxed can transport you through your day, manifesting a positive attitude in everything you do. Others will see you as cheerful and energetic and will respond positively to you. Issues that may have upset you when you were more tense will seem less stressful.

Thought Stopping

It is well documented that only one thought can occupy your mind at once. The concept of thought stopping is based on the theory that we are all engaged in self-talk during our waking hours. If we can only have one thought at a time, it will change our thinking if we stop negative thoughts from starting. Notice when a disruptive thought comes to your mind and either picture a stop sign or mentally say to your self, "STOP." Sometimes a rubber band around the wrist can be used to snap and interrupt a negative thought when it comes to mind. With enough interruption of negative thoughts you can learn to prevent them from continuously controlling your behavior.

This behavior interruption received a lot of publicity when it was implemented by the American Lung Association in some of their anti-smoking classes as being an effective means in aiding people to quit cigarettes.

Refuting Irrational Ideas

Since all of us engage in continuous self-talk, an internal language we use to describe and interpret the world, we need to attack our irrational ideas and beliefs as soon as we think them. When self-talk is realistic and accurate, wellness is enhanced. When self-talk is irrational and untrue, stress and emotional disturbance occur.

Psychologist Albert Ellis developed a system to attack irrational ideas or beliefs and replace them with more realistic ones. Irrational self-talk is apt to lead to unpleasant emotions, and unpleasant emotions can lead to an escalation of the physical symptoms we know as anxiety.

Rational self-talk tends to lead to pleasant feelings and a positive interpretation of experience.

A common form of irrational self-talk includes making events more catastrophic and nightmarish than they actually are. Examples of this kind of self-talk are: wondering if that momentary chest pain is a heart attack, or that a grumpy word from your supervisor at work means you are about to be fired.

Some of the statements that many of us either think or say that Ellis considered irrational are:

It is easier to avoid difficulty than to face it.

Unfamiliar situations always lead to anxiety and fear.

People are helpless. People have no control over what happens to them.

Good relationships are built on sacrifice.

There is only one perfect love.

A person can only be judged by their achievements.

Anger is bad.

Perhaps you have thought some of these things yourself. But in order to decrease your anxiety level, you need to develop some skills in refuting irrational ideas. The following is an example of a practice to develop the skills necessary to be more rational in the way you approach stressful situations.

1. Write down the facts of some stressful event, including what you saw everyone involved do: detail their behavior. Leave out any judgements or analysis you might have made at the time. (She was so mean, I could hardly stand it.) (He just stood there with his mouth hanging open, looking stupid.) (I know we are all going to get fired because of this, and it's not my fault.)

2. Write down your self-talk at the time. This is the place for your judgments, beliefs, predictions and worries.

3. Examine your original analysis of the event for any irrational belief.

4. Write down your emotional response to the event, such as: angry, hopeless, fearful.

5. From your list of irrational statements, choose one to refute.

6. List your evidence that the statement might be false or irrational.

7. Write the worst thing that could happen as a result of this event.

8. Write down the good things that could happen as the result of the worst thing happening.

9. Re-write your self-talk, making it more positive and up-beat.

An example of performing this exercise, so you might understand how it would be helpful to you:

1. Event: Another employee complained to the boss about a mistake you made.

2. Self-talk: "I hate him. I ought to strangle him. How could he have done that? I could lose my job! What will I do, how will I pay the mortgage!"

3. Irrational: You know you really couldn't strangle anyone. One mistake won't cause you to lose your job. The mortgage is not due for another 30 days.

4. Emotional response: Furious.

5. Refute: "I ought to strangle him." If I actually strangled him, things would only be worse. The error would still be there, I would not only lose my job, I'd go to jail--and the mortgage would never get paid.

6. Rational thought: I did make one mistake but I learned from it. I can handle explaining it. Not only did it make me aware of something I overlooked, it was a learning experience. Working with him is unpleasant, but I can deal with it.

7. Mislabeling of emotions: Mislabeling own embarrassment as hate and anger.

8. Worst thing: I could really retaliate.

9. Best thing: Work was getting sloppy because my mind was elsewhere. This will make me more careful.

10. Alternate thought: Nothing really terrible happened. I can handle this.

11. Alternative emotion: I'm not really furious, I'm just annoyed.

Coping Skills

Coping skills are very similar to assertiveness training. They are statements which can be rehearsed prior to a tense situation or can be used during an uncomfortable encounter. They work well as preparation in combination with structured relaxation. Some examples might be: You have made an error. You begin by performing some abdominal breathing. Instead of running though a list of "what if's" in your head, you begin self-talk in a positive manner. This can be rehearsed before hand for specific situations that you know always cause you stress or generically for the types of stress that increase your anxiety. Self-talk: This will be over soon. I can handle it. I can do this. I will be calm and think through the steps carefully. I will slow down and take my time.

One of the problems is that phobic individuals are masters of visualization but what they usually visualize are catastrophes.

Dr. Victoria Johnson, director of the Phobia Center in Marin County, California, offered a 12-week group program in thought stopping. She demonstrates, "For example: If you drive down the road thinking, 'Gee, I feel a little nervous. What if I get so nervous I won't be able to drive? What if I crash the car? What if I go crazy and jump out of the car while it's moving?' Phobic individuals can take this kind of thinking on and on until they are hyperventilating, sweating and shaking. But it is possible to replace this kind of catastrophic thinking with positive thoughts." She goes on, "You probably drive very well even when you are anxious. In fourteen years of working with phobic individuals, I have never heard of anyone who had an accident because of their disorder. Drive the road, not your emotions."

In addition, Dr. Johnson says, "Examine yourself. Does your chest feel tight? Take a deep breath. Are you gripping the wheel tightly? Relax your hands. Are you staring straight ahead, too scared to look left or right? Deliberately scan the road from side to side. Practice diaphragmatic breathing."

Dr. Johnson usually begins with several weeks of classroom learning about relaxation techniques and thought stopping and then she begins the field work. "There is no blinding flash of light and everything is solved. Fear gradually drops away if you work at it. Decide that this is your most important job right now, and work at it."

Managing Time

Everyone has only twenty-four hours in each day. Some individuals manage to handle the day's tasks easily, some become stressed when they think they cannot accomplish all that they would like to. Time management skills are an essential foundation to managing stress, because they allow time to practice all the other techniques. Three basic time management skills are: priority setting, the elimination of low priority tasks and decision making.

While you attempt to whittle down the stress you are subjected to daily:

> Learn to say "no" (it is possible that this may require enrolling in a course of assertiveness training);
>
> Build time into your schedule for interruptions and unforeseen occurrences;
>
> Set aside time during the day for structured relaxation or listening to relaxation tapes. A relaxed person is more productive.

Exercise

A healthy body tolerates all kinds of stress much better than an unhealthy one. This is even more true for those with a highly reactive nervous system. Regular exercise oxygenates the blood and the brain, increasing alertness and concentration. In addition, it oxidizes substances it doesn't need, including lactic acid. If you begin an exercise program, begin slowly, very slowly. Any increase in lactic acid should be offset by your body's increased ability to handle it.

For a few, the increase in lactate in the blood has been shown to increase panic attack response and, for those individuals, an aerobic exercise such as easy walking, Hatha Yoga or Tai Chi, the slow muscle strengthening exercise of the Chinese, are excellent examples of exercise which will result in releasing muscle tension without rapidly or greatly elevating lactate levels. For those who are able to tolerate exercise, plan to make exercise part of your weekly routine. Any aerobic exercise, three times a week for at least twenty minutes each session, can increase your ability to deal with stress and reduce muscle tension and anxiety.

For those who are unable to tolerate exercise and for those who are still bothered by anxiety disorder even after mild exercise, psychotherapy, biofeedback, cognitive and relaxation techniques or short-term pharmacotherapy may be necessary before an exercise program can be undertaken.

Exercise is a natural way to elevate endorphins, opiate-like compounds which are the body's natural pain killers. The "runner's high" is one well known phenomenon that results from elevating endorphins through exercise.

There are many good books available on exercise and a great variety of exercise programs available on video tape and television.

Of course, before beginning any exercise program, particularly if you have been sedentary, it is wise to check with your doctor.

The non-prescription treatment dimethylglycine, taken during and after physical exertion, can prevent or at least reduce the buildup of lactic acid for those who have panic attacks as the result of lactic acid buildup in the blood.

The benzodiazepines are effective in treating generalized anxiety disorders. The shorter-acting drugs usually provide quick relief but do not sustain their effectiveness, while the longer-acting medications will not produce immediate relief from symptoms but will maintain their effects over a longer period.

These medications are safe when used alone but when combined with alcohol, they can become lethal. While these drugs may enable an individual to undertake an exercise program, they only relieve symptoms. They do nothing to affect any underlying cause and should only be a temporary remedy to anxiety.

Nutrition

If you eat a lot of processed foods, frozen dinners, fast-food restaurant meals or follow low-calorie diets, you may be shortchanging your body and your brain. You probably don't realize it, but continually drinking coffee or soft drinks or missing meals weakens your body's natural resistance to anxiety. During periods of stress it is particularly important to bolster your diet by eating balanced meals every day and possibly adding a vitamin supplement.

"Most people I have talked to say they had their first panic attack during a stressful time in their lives," says Shirley Swede. "Chances are, they were run-down physically--people don't realize their bodies need more nutrients when they are under stress."

You can boost your energy and improve your emotional outlook by making some simple changes in your eating habits. Many who are fatigued, depressed and anxious are suffering from an imbalance of nutrients and a deficiency in vitamins, minerals and amino acids.

For some, the highly reactive state which is accompanied by the physical symptoms of anxiety, panic attack and phobias may be the result of the body reaching the breaking point due to excessive stress from physical illness, injury, relationship or work-related problems or an unhealthy life-style.

You must learn how to adjust to the fact that your body reacts more strongly than the average body when it is overstressed. A strong healthy body tolerates stress much better than an unhealthy one. To increase your body's ability to tolerate stress you need a well-balanced diet. The diabetic has to learn how to control food intake to keep this disease under control and so do the highly anxious.

A well-balanced diet builds stress resistance in a number of ways. It increases physical endurance, increases resistance to disease and promotes increased emotional stability. Unfortunately, for many of us, the first thing to suffer during periods of excessive stress is most often the diet.

Stress and anxiety tend to interfere with the digestive system, which decreases its activity during the fight or flight response. In addition, those foods which have a low nutritional content but often have a high emotional value, such as chocolate or sugary treats, are quite often used as a coping device. When the diet goes by the wayside during anxiety attacks the body is less able to resist the effects of stress and that results in increased anxiety.

Excessive sugar can produce mood swings. A classic book on the subject, which should be read by everyone who has turned to sweets in moments of anxiety, is *Body, Mind & Sugar* by E. M. Abrahamson,

M.D. But don't just avoid the obvious sources of sugar, such as ice cream, cake and alcohol. Read labels on processed and packaged foods, because sugar may be an ingredient disguised as fructose, glucose, sucrose, dextrose, natural sweeteners and syrups.

The body or the brain can be likened to a machine: without proper fuel it does not run well or efficiently. It is not necessary to count calories and grams of fat and carbohydrates to be well nourished. There are hundreds of books or nutrition and well-balanced meals in any book store or library. However, those with highly-reactive nervous system should avoid fad diets or those diets which are likely to put additional stress on the nervous system.

Eat more fruits, vegetables and grains, nuts and seeds. Each day, you should aim for a minimum of two servings of fruit, three servings of vegetables, two servings of grains and two servings of nuts and seeds.

At least one serving of vegetables should be dark green or yellow. Another serving should be a vegetable from the cabbage family, such as broccoli, brussels sprouts or cauliflower.

When you purchase cereal, bread, pasta and rice, look for the words "whole grain" on the label.

Serve cooked beans several times a week. Beans

provide carbohydrates, as well as nature's most complete vegetable protein.

Limit your protein to no more than one egg for breakfast and four-ounce servings of meat or fish for lunch and dinner. Replace the protein with more vegetables and whole grains. And limit meats to lean cuts and trim all visible fat.

Instead of using mayonnaise, sour cream and other whole-milk or creamy products, substitute skim milk, nonfat yogurt and low-fat cheese.

Most people, even without any anxiety difficulties, will feel better on such a diet within two months.

When you are experiencing a period of high stress, pay strict attention to your diet. In addition, if you know that you are facing a stressful day, pay extra attention to seeing that your body and brain are well nourished.

Food cravings are well known to have a mood connection. Women typically crave sugar-fat combinations. Eating sugars and starches increases the presence in the brain of serotonin, that brain chemical that is the body's own natural antidepressant.

Fat cravings may be a need to stimulate endorphins, those opiate-like compounds that are the body's natural pain-killers and are triggered by eating fats. When endorphin levels are low you will feel anxious, depressed and your appetite for fat (as well as sugar) is activated. These dietary antistress foods give a temporary endorphin lift plus a serotonin lift. But beware, there is a backlash effect, particularly damaging to those suffering from panic disorder and that is the downside of raising blood levels of sugar and fat excessively, only to have them fall drastically a few hours later.

Hoffer and Walker, authors of *Orthomolecular Nutrition*, state:

> Every tissue of the body is affected by nutrition. Under conditions of poor nutrition the kidney stops filtering, the stomach stops digesting, the adrenals stop secreting and other organs follow suit. Unfortunately, some psychiatrists labor under the false belief that somehow brain function is completely unaffected by nutrition.

Living Well

Managing Conflict and Fear

When the things you want and need interfere with what someone else wants and needs there is conflict. Since every person wants and needs something different, conflict is natural in all human relationships. However, you may find any kind of conflict difficult and that can be a very major source of anxiety and stress in human relationships.

For those who were raised in the homes with abusive or alcoholic parents or adults, or in homes where there are very rigid views concerning behavior, conflict was something you probably learned to try to avoid at any cost.

There are four basic types of behavior possible when faced with a conflicting situation: passive, passive-aggressive, aggressive and assertive.

Passive behavior

The non-assertive or passive person's main goal is to avoid conflict and often to do that you must place the needs and wants of others before your own. You may often allow others to make choices for you and take advantage of you. Very often non-assertive behavior is in response to authority figures, such as supervisors, teachers or parents and in proper situations, may be appropriate.

When you do not stand up for your rights or do not take action to satisfy your needs and wants because they conflict with the needs and wants of others, you are being non-assertive. While this is appropriate in some situations, the frequent, habitual use of non-assertive behavior usually causes you to lose self-respect and self-esteem. It is very difficult to think highly of yourself when your needs are not being met and when others disregard your dignity and ignore your needs. With enough non-assertive behavior on your part, you become a door-mat, losing the respect of the person for whom you are abrogating your rights.

The woman who works to put her husband through school, who does without items she needs to pay tuition, who never has anything new to wear because his clothing needs come first, who defers to his needs for privacy or quiet in order to study, who takes the kids out of the house to the park to play for fear they are making too much noise; may find that, when he finally graduates, he will find her too boring and leave her for a woman he then meets in his new career. This is a well known scenario to many a woman who spent many years "putting hubby through," only to find that she had given up too much of herself through such non-assertive helping behavior.

Passive-aggressive behavior

Such non-assertive behavior sometimes results in passive-aggressive behavior. This is the "getting back" at someone indirectly such as by forgetting an important meeting or being late for appointments. Another form of passive-aggressive behavior is manipulation. When people are unable to fulfill needs and wants in a direct manner they sometimes will sulk or cry to get their way because they cannot state up-front what it is they want. The flirtatious begging that is used to get someone to do something is another example of manipulative behavior that is childish and unattractive, but many non-assertive people find it effective when they fear being confrontational.

Non-assertiveness can result in blaming. The inability to take responsibility for the quality of your life may result in blaming others for your problems. Long-term non-assertive behavior sometimes is observed in martyr-type personalities. The spouse of an alcoholic who covers up, makes excuses, and then blames the alcoholic's drinking for all the problems in a relationship is an example of a passive-aggressive person.

Whenever you choose non-assertive behavior, you elect to have irritation within yourself in order to avoid irritation in a relationship. This encourages more unwanted behavior from others and it prevents relationships from going forward.

Aggressive behavior

Aggressive behavior has a very straight-forward goal--to gain control. When you are aggressive, you express your needs and wants directly but in a hostile, tactless or angry manner. There is no doubt in the other individual's mind what it is that you want. This is standing up for your wants and needs, but it is ignoring the wants and needs of others if they interfere with yours.

There are some occasions when aggresive behavior is appropriate, such as when there is immi-
nent danger to life or property.

Most of the time aggressive behavior is as self-
defeating as non-assertive behavior. Others who are
the object of aggressive behavior usually feel as if
they are being attacked. Sometimes they feel intimi-
dated and they do what is wanted and sometimes
they fight back, even if most of the time this is not
their style. However, aggressive behavior causes both
people to become more hostile and to resist cooper-
ating or helping. Most very aggressive individuals are
avoided by others. As a result, aggressive people are
often without friends because they are frightening.
And, as unlikely as it might seem to non-aggressive
individuals, the aggressive person may feel guilty and
sad after mistreating others and failing to solve their
conflict by aggression.

Assertive behavior

The goal of assertive behavior is to resolve conflicts in a way that is satisfying to both you and
others involved. When you are assertive you express
problems, feelings, needs and wants in a way that is
both self-satisfying and socially effective. You respect
the rights and dignity of both yourself and others.
There is personal focus on reasonable compromise
rather than on winning. Solutions to problems are

those which will make everyone feel good about the outcome.

Many people think that aggressive and assertive behavior are the same. This confusion seems to come from the fact that much is said and written about changing from non-assertive behavior and becoming assertive to get what you want. Very little is written about changing aggressive behavior to assertive behavior. Both assertive and aggressive styles involve expressing yourself freely, standing up for your rights, and working to satisfy your needs and wants. However, the difference is that an aggressive approach ignores the rights and needs of others.

Anger often gets in the way of being assertive. The angrier you are, the more aggressively you will behave. When you are accustomed to behaving non-assertively, it means that you allow others to take advantage of or be mean to you regularly. And then, when you have had all you can take, you get angry and lose control, lashing out. Such aggression will probably startle those who are unaccustomed to such behavior from you. Whatever their reaction, conflict can arise from such a "scene," with resulting guilt and shame and more internal conflict for you.

Individuals with anxiety, phobias and panic disorder often think that they may not be able to handle a situation, will look stupid, could get their feelings hurt, be taken advantage of, be a failure, might lose control, and a myriad of things if they change their behavioral style to become assertive. The result of such thinking is stress which then generates anxiety.

In fact, being assertive means that you believe in both your individual rights and the rights of others.

If your behavioral style is regularly anything other than assertive, you need to make the effort to change that, whether through taking a course on assertiveness or recognizing that your inter-personal style is creating some of the stress in your life and practicing different ways of being in conflict situations.

Many people resort to self-medication to avoid conflict, and the result of such self-medication is twofold. First, the conflict is usually not resolved satisfactorily, adding to your stress. And second, the self-medication can result in dependency as well as poor conflict-resolution behavior.

Remember, there is no such thing as a tranquilizer deficiency! The chemicals in tranquilizers do replicate many of the neurotransmitters and neurotransmitter blockers of nature. But, if you wish to avoid drugs, take control of your life, try nature's remedies instead.

Diet

It is best to eat a proper diet and then supplement the diet with a good assortment of minerals and vitamins.

Roger J. Williams in *Nutrition Against Disease* describes an adequate diet as follows:

Amino acids

Amino acids are the building blocks for proteins. They are essential for a number of reasons: they build body tissues; they supply food fuel for the body whenever insufficient fats and carbohydrates are consumed; they help maintain normal blood sugar; they assist in the transport of various minerals and vitamins and they assist in the acid-base balance of the body. Protein is needed for the health and formation of muscles, hormones, membranes, glands, enzymes, skin, plasma, teeth, antibodies, ligaments, hair, fingernails, bones, cartilage, hemoglobin, brain and nerve cells.

Vitamins B and C

Vitamin B is actually a complex of several vitamins, including B-1, B-2, B-3, B-6 and B-12, PABA, as well as folic acid, choline and inositol. These are water soluble vitamins which means they are not stored in the body and therefore must be supplied in sufficient amounts at all times--especially when the body is under stress.

Even through the B vitamins should be supplied in the diet in quantities sufficient to support normal health, this supply can be inadequate under stress. Stress is anything that causes extra tension--emotional or physical, such as drugs, alcohol, chemicals, excessive fatigue, noise, infections, anxiety.

The B vitamins are found in whole grain cereals and breads, dark green leafy vegetables, beans and soy beans, brewer's yeast, wheat germ, poultry, beef and liver.

Vitamin C, another water soluble vitamin, is essential to the body for the formation of collagen in the body; collagen is a protein substance that cements the cells of the body together to make tissue. It is important and necessary for the development of healthy capillaries, bones, cartilage, teeth and connective tissue; to protect the body from infection; aid the adrenals in production of cortisone; to assist in the absorption of iron from the intestines.

This vitamin is an antioxidant; it helps to neutralize foreign substances, chemicals and poisons in the body. The body's need for Vitamin C increases greatly during times of stress; again, this is stress in any form--emotional, physical, such as during an infection.

Without Vitamin C we would have scurvy, a disease that was common in sailors on sailing vessels who were at sea for lengthy periods at a time and had no access to fresh fruit. However, minor forms of this disease can be seen in bleeding gums, the tendency to bruise easily, tendency to sinus infections, allergies and hay fever.

Vitamin C is present in citrus fruits and dark green-leafy vegetables.

Vitamins A, D and E

These three vitamins are fat soluble, that is, fat is necessary in the diet for these vitamins to be properly absorbed by the body.

Vitamin A is an antioxidant which contributes to sight, resistance to infections, and the maintenance of healthy skin, bones and mucous membranes.

Vitamin D is called the sunshine vitamin because exposure to the rays of the sun produces this vitamin which is then stored in the liver. It is needed for the body to properly utilize calcium and phosphorus which are both important for strong bones and teeth.

Vitamin E is an antioxidant and it plays a role in the protection of Vitamin A, as well as other body fats.

Vitamin A is widely distributed in yellow vegetables and fruits such as carrots, cantaloupe, sweet potatoes, apricots, dark green leafy vegetables, eggs, milk, fish liver oils and liver.

Vitamin D can be found in fish liver oils, eggs and fortified milk.

Vitamin E is available from vegetables, oils, grains, eggs, liver and meat.

The minerals

Vitamins cannot function without the assistance of minerals. Minerals work together as a group rather than individually. They work in conjunction with hormones, enzymes, proteins, carbohydrates, fats and vitamins. They are required for the proper overall mental and physical function of the body and they help to build and maintain the entire structure.

Calcium is the most abundant mineral in the body. About 99 percent of the calcium in the body is found in the bones and teeth, the other one percent is in the soft tissues and blood--this lowly one percent has a great impact on the nerves. It is found in milk, dairy products, leafy green vegetables, cereal and bread.

Magnesium is a natural tranquilizer for the nervous system. It is needed for protein and carbohydrate metabolism. Signs of magnesium deficiency are similar to a hangover: noise sensitivity, tremors, twitching, rapid heartbeat, aching muscles, fatigue, depression, and irritability. It is the only electrolyte which has a higher level in the brain fluid than in the blood plasma. It is available from whole grain breads and cereals, green leafy vegetables and milk.

Potassium is vital for the proper functioning of

nerves, heart and muscles. In addition, it works with sodium to maintain the body's water-salt balance.

Phosphorus is important in nearly all physiological chemical reactions within the body. It is necessary for normal bone and tooth structure and for the transmission of nerve impulses and is necessary for the metabolism of fats and carbohydrates.

Iron is found in the red blood cells as part of the hemoglobin and hemoglobin is the protein that carries oxygen to the body tissues. Its sources include whole grain cereals and breads, wheat germ, dark green leafy vegetables and beans, eggs, liver and meat.

Zinc is involved in many enzyme systems. Zinc is essential for healthy hair, appetite, sense of taste and energy. It is available from seafood, kelp and iodized table salt.

The remaining minerals have a number of complex enzymatic functions in the monitoring and repair of body systems and are found in either a multi-mineral tablet or in a varied diet. Because there are other obscure nutrients such as phenols, flavones and lutein which science does not as yet fully understand, it is necessary to eat a diet rich in a variety of fruits and vegetables.

Chronic stress, whether environmental, physical or resulting from strenuous exercise or physical activity, often results in a need for the 'anti-stress' vitamins, B and C. The B vitamins and C are rapidly utilized any time the body is stressed.

Sleep

Chronic sleeplessness can increase anxiety symptoms and interfere with health, relationships, and the ability to function effectively. Because chronic sleep problems may be due to either a medication or medical problem, it is best to discuss sleep problems with your physician. Difficulty in sleeping is quite often due to poor bedtime habits or thinking patterns which interfere with the ability to go to sleep.

If your sleep is poor or interrupted or you waken early feeling fatigued, it is possible the problem may be depression and should be discussed with your doctor.

Sleeping medications are habit forming, are only for short-term sleeplessness, and should only be taken after attempts have been made to improve your bedtime habits. Prescription sleeping medications can alter normal sleeping patterns and suppress REM sleep. They will also leave you feeling groggy the following day. The body becomes tolerant to some forms of these drugs and higher and higher doses become necessary, leading to dependency. Quite often, the use of prescription sleeping pills for a short-term period of sleeplessness can lead to long-term sleep problems.

Melatonin is lowered in the morning by light, and darkness increases melatonin levels, the brain chemical that regulates our sleep cycles. Maintain a healthy internal biological clock. Go to bed and arise at the same time each day and do not sleep-in on the weekends or days off. Naps are all right if they are taken early enough in the day, are not for more than thirty minutes and do not appear to be the cause of sleeplessness.

If you are a shift worker and must make schedule changes do so gradually. One week before the change, go to bed an hour earlier each night in a darkened room. At the beginning of the week you may have a little trouble going right to sleep but by the end of the week you should be awaking refreshed for your shift.

Avoid stimulants for three to five hours before bedtime. Caffeine and heavy meals are not beneficial to good sleep. Avoid alcohol. While many think of alcohol as a relaxing drug, even moderate amounts of alcohol can disrupt sleep and often causes a backlash of sleeplessness in the early morning hours.

Reserve your bed for sleeping and sex. If you read, watch exciting television, eat, or work crossword puzzles in bed, you are setting up a subconscious concept that your bed is for all kinds of other activities.

Make the bedroom inviting to sleep in. Make the window treatments heavy enough to keep out light and noise. It is easier to fall asleep in a room that is dark, quiet and well ventilated.

Establish a bedtime routine by setting up a conditioned response. If you regularly wash your face, brush your teeth, set out your clothing for the next day, wind the clock, walk the dog, put out the cat; do all these things in a regular, routine order. This will become your conditioned response that triggers your body to go to sleep after these things are finished. Whatever activities you choose for your conditioned response, such a hot bath, praying or meditating, remember to choose only relaxing activities. Avoid anxiety-arousing activities such as paying bills, watching horror movies or loud, energizing music.

If you go to bed and find that you cannot fall asleep, do not stay in bed worrying about the fact that you cannot get to sleep. After no more than twenty minutes, get up, do something that you regularly find relaxing in some other part of the house. Read or watch television, or some other quiet activity until you begin to feel sleepy. Only then should you go back to bed.

Exercise just before attempting to sleep will interfere with sleep. Three to five hours before bedtime, heavy exercise will interfere with your ability to sleep. However, light exercise, such as a walk around the block after dinner, will improve the amount of good sleep in the early part of the night.

If you have been unable to sleep and then find that you are so. .o. .o sleepy in the afternoon, change your activity. Get out of your chair. Move, stretch. Be creative--try a piece of fruit, herb tea or water breaks and brief walks in place of cigarettes, alcohol and coffee.

Lying in bed worrying about the "what ifs" and the "if only I had saids" will definitely keep you awake, even if you are physically exhausted. Get up, go to another room and make a creative plan to deal with that something you are worrying about. If this is a future event, role play the various things you think could or might happen, and decide how you will handle them. Visualize yourself handling the difficulty well. Once you have done this, go back to bed and practice one of your relaxation techniques. If you find yourself drifting back to thinking about the problem, repeat your creative plan to yourself and resume your relaxation exercise.

If you find that you routinely do this type of worrying once you go to bed to sleep then establish a time before going to bed to formulate a creative plan. Once you are in bed with a plan well thought out, use relaxation techniques to assist you to sleep.

If you find that you awaken in the middle of the night worrying about something and can't get back to sleep, get up, go to another room and do something calming before attempting to go back to sleep.

Some people are awakened by a panic attack in the middle of the night which leaves them in a state of high anxiety. If you do have sleep time panic attacks but are able to go back to sleep, do whatever it is that relaxes you and return to sleep.

If however, you find that night time panic attacks trigger all the "what ifs" that you can possibly imagine and that you have a difficult time going back to sleep, try the following:

Get out of bed. Awaken yourself by putting water on your face. Once you are completely awake, describe to yourself exactly what happened. This is an excellent time to begin to identify feelings. Often sufferers of panic disorder find that their internal feelings are so uncomfortable that they push them away in an effort to feel better. Some people over eat to avoid feelings, others stuff their feelings down or create a crisis to distract themselves from distressing internal responses. Stuffed feelings can turn into panic attacks.

When awakened in the middle of the night, it is a good time to take a look at the fact that panic signals you need to heal your pain.

Even though you are unaware of your feelings, your body stores memories and the feelings associated with them until they are processed. Tense body muscles reflect repressed unconscious conflicts and feelings. If you are tight and tense, it is more difficult to identify your reactions. When you deny these feelings, they get stronger in your unconscious, building up pressure.

Once you can name your emotions, they are easier to identify and experience. Notice your internal dialogue and make a short list of the feelings you may have thought of at the moment of awakening. List them before you return to bed. In the morning reexamine the list you have noted during the night. See if there are words such as love, affection, concern, joy, depression, distress, fear, anxiety, inadequacy, anger, hostility on your list. As you examine it, you may find that words that describe the first four emotions (love, affection, concern, joy) are missing. Think about what you can do to add these experiences to your life.

You know from prior experience with panic attacks what the physical symptoms are and that they will pass. While these feelings are very uncomfortable and frightening, you know that they will pass.

Take the time during the night to engage in a brief relaxing activity, such as reading, listening to calming music and having a cup of warm milk. It is helpful to have things prepared ahead of time. Have one of your relaxation tapes on the tape player. Have something out to heat the milk in should you think you want it. Have something available to read that is calming, such as a book of poetry. This should take no more than ten minutes, in which time you will allow the physical symptoms to quiet. Go back to bed and practice one of your relaxation techniques.

The New "What-Ifs"

You have decided that you are not going to live with anxiety, phobia or panic anymore--you are going to take charge of your life--and the old "what-ifs" of dread, fear and terror are to be in your past. The new "what-ifs" are your present reality: the "what-ifs" of your life free of dread, terror and fear. Now you are thinking: what if I enjoy myself? What if I get a promotion at work? What if I take an adventurous vacation? The fears are dropping out of your life because of increased assertiveness and independence. This is all part of a process of recovery. You are formulating new goals for your life now, perhaps going back to school and fulfilling life-long dreams. As you make these changes in your world and become more confident of your recovery, seek out joy and pleasure in your daily activities. As you do so remember that just as you created body chemistry with old destructive thinking, you are now creating beneficial body chemistry with every new and positive thought.

You will no longer be trapped in your old unrealistic mode. The future is good and your new found freedom will bring to you a better life than you ever thought possible. Work on the new ways of living and the new "what-ifs" daily and you will have mastery over panic.

Where to Find More Help

WHEN ONE MEMBER OF A FAMILY HAS PANIC DISORDER, the entire family is affected by the condition. Family members may be frustrated in their attempts to help the affected person cope with the disorder, over-burdened by taking on additional responsibilities, and socially isolated. Family members must encourage the person with panic disorder to seek the help of a qualified mental health professional, if needed.

Also, it is often helpful for family members to attend an occasional treatment or self-help session or seek the guidance of a therapist in dealing with their feelings about the disorder.

For more information on panic disorder and related conditions:

American Psychiatric Association
1400 K. Street, N.W.
Washington, DC 20005
(202) 682-6220

American Psychological Association
750 First Street, N.E.
Washington, DC 20002
(202) 336-5800

Anxiety Disorders Association of America
600 Executive Blvd., Suite 513
Rockville, MD 20852
1-900-737-3400

Association for the Advancement of Behavior
   Therapy
25 West 36th Street
New York, NY 10018
(212) 379-7970

National Anxiety Foundation
3135 Custer Drive
Lexington, KY 40517-4001
1-800-755-1576

National Depressive and Manic Depressive
   Association
740 North Franklin Street
Suite 501
Chicago, IL 60601

National Institute of Mental Health
Publications List
5600 Fishers Lane
Room 15C-05
Rockville, MD 20857

National Mental Health Association
1201 Prince Street
Alexandria, VA 22314-29710
(703)684-7722

American Academy of Child and Adolescent
   Psychiatry
3615 Wisconsin Avenue, N.W.
Washington, DC 20016
(202) 966-7300

For obsessive-compulsive information:

Dean Foundation
8000 Excelsior Drive, Suite 203
Madison, WI 53717

OCD Biological Studies Program
Department of Psychiatry
Columbia Presbyterian Medical Center
722 West 168th Street
New York, NY 10032

Ultimately, the person with any disorder must be responsible for controlling his or her own condition. However, it may be necessary to seek help from a therapist for assistance until you are well enough to take over that control.

Often the person with panic disorder must undertake a strenuous search to find a therapist who is familiar with the most effective treatments for the condition. The Anxiety Disorders Association of America can provide a list of professionals in your area who specialize in the treatment of panic disorder and other anxiety disorders.

Self-help and support groups are the least expensive approach to managing panic disorder, and are helpful for many people. A group of about 5 to 10 people meet weekly and share their experiences, encouraging each other to venture into feared situations and cope effectively with panic attacks. Group members are in charge of the sessions. Often family members are invited to attend these groups and at times a therapist or other panic disorder expert may be brought in to share insights with group members. Information on self-help groups in specific areas of the country can be obtained from the Anxiety Disorders Association of America.

In addition, help can be found in the Yellow Pages of the telephone directory under: *Mental Health, Health, Anxiety, Suicide Prevention, Hospitals, Physicians, Psychiatrists, Psychologists,* or *Social Workers.* You can also find referrals, diagnostic and treatment services from: family doctors, mental health specialists, health maintenance organizations, community mental health centers, hospital psychiatry departments and outpatient clinics, University- or medical school-affiliated programs and clinics, state hospital outpatient clinics, family service/social agencies, private clinics and facilities, employee assistance programs and local medical, psychiatric, or psychological societies or associations.

Index

A

Abdominal breathing, 259-260
Abuse, 143-144
ACTH, 74
Adenosine, 105-106
Adjustment disorders, 213
Adolescence, 137
　personality development,
　　139-140
Adrenal glands, 74
Adrenaline, 21
　PMS and, 241
Adrenaline response, 180, 181
Adrenocorticotrophic
　hormone, 74
Adult role, child assuming, 146
Aerobic exercise, 282
Agoraphobia, 58-60, 106, 127,
　214
Albuterol, 100
Alcohol, 103-105, 251-252, 301
Alcohol abuse, 143, 178, 190
　panic attack and, 31
　post-traumatic stress and,
　　245
Alprazolam, 205
American Academy of Child and
　Adolescent Psychiatry, 311
American Psychiatric Associa-
　tion, 309
Amino acids, 187-190, 295
Amitriptyline, 205
Amphetamines, 102
Anafranil, 206, 243
Anger, 293
Animal studies, 126-127
Anterior pituitary gland, 75

Anti-inflammatories, 100
Anticipatory anxiety, 30-31, 39
Antidepressants, 100, 204, 206
Antioxidant, 297
Anxiety, 13, 180, 234-237
　alcohol and, 13
　anticipatory, 30-31, 39
　brain chemistry and, 20
　childhood and, 20
　generalized, 36-37
　high, development of, 142-
　　146
　men and, 13
　phobia vs, 15
　problem solving and, 153
　symptoms of, 36-37
　women and, 13, 31
Anxiety Disorders Association
　of America, 310, 311, 312
Aspartame, 108
Assertive behavior, 292-294,
　294
Association for the Advance-
　ment of Behavior Therapy,
　310
Asthma, 94
Atenolol, 205
Ativan, 188, 205
Augustus Caesar, 3

B

Bedtime routine, 302
Behavioral-cognitive therapy,
　220
Benzodiazepines, 124, 205, 283
Beta-blockers, 205
Bicarbonate ions, 176

313

NOTES

NOTES

NOTES

NOTES

NOTES

NOTES

NOTES

NOTES

NOTES

NOTES